STRUCTURALISM

SYNTHESE LIBRARY

MONOGRAPHS ON EPISTEMOLOGY,

LOGIC, METHODOLOGY, PHILOSOPHY OF SCIENCE,

SOCIOLOGY OF SCIENCE AND OF KNOWLEDGE,

AND ON THE MATHEMATICAL METHODS OF

SOCIAL AND BEHAVIORAL SCIENCES

Editors:

ROBERT S. COHEN, *Boston University*

DONALD DAVIDSON, *Rockefeller University and Princeton University*

JAAKKO HINTIKKA, *Academy of Finland and Stanford University*

GABRIËL NUCHELMANS, *University of Leyden*

WESLEY C. SALMON, *University of Arizona*

VOLUME 67

JAN M. BROEKMAN

STRUCTURALISM

Moscow – Prague – Paris

D. REIDEL PUBLISHING COMPANY

DORDRECHT-HOLLAND / BOSTON-U.S.A.

First printing: December 1974

STRUKTURALISMUS

First published in 1971 by Verlag Karl Aller, Freiburg/München
Translated from the German by Jan F. Beekman and Brunhilde Helm

Library of Congress Catalog Card Number 74–79570

ISBN 90 277 0478 3

Published by D. Reidel Publishing Company,
P.O. Box 17, Dordrecht, Holland

Sold and distributed in the U.S.A., Canada, and Mexico
by D. Reidel Publishing Company, Inc.
306 Dartmouth Street, Boston,
Mass. 02116, U.S.A.

Printed in The Netherlands

TABLE OF CONTENTS

PREFACE TO THE ENGLISH EDITION

The use of the word 'structuralism', not only as a title for the present book but also as a valuable indication for outstanding philosophical and cultural developments of our century, may embarrass the English reader. The same might be the case regarding some of the philosophical thoughts developed in connexion with this structuralism. Emphasis is namely not on a set of technical operations using ideas and conceptions closely linked up with 'structural' or 'systematical' analyses, system and information theories, biology, psychology and even literary criticism. On the contrary, the concept of structuralism here definitely refers to a holistic approach, not unlike existentialism or phenomenology. Many philosophical implications of this structuralism are however quite different from those contained in existential philosophies. The first difference applies to philosophy itself: no existential thinker will doubt or deny that the thoughts developed are genuine philosophical thoughts. Structuralism however does not take that decision beforehand, and thus no longer restricts itself to the traditional laws and habits of philosophical reasoning. It presents itself on the one hand as a holistic attempt to interpret reality among lines of philosophical argumentation, but tries to do so without the decision that this argumentation leads to philosophy. Structuralism therefore presents itself as a specific *activity*, a *modus operandi* in reality itself. In consequence, the philosophical implications of this operation are to be analyzed in the same way, but they are only elements of the total structuralistic discourse, a discourse that extends to anthropology, psychology, linguistics, aesthetics, and other fields rather than interpreting itself as philosophical in the traditional sense of the word.

This idea is clearly rooted in general cultural developments covering many fields and a wide variety of interests. This becomes clear after a closer examination of Russian aesthetics in Formalism, Marxism, Futurism, or Romanticism; in French Cubism, Italian Futurism, or Czech structural linguistics; not to mention intertwining developments in phonology, ethnology, mathematics, or biology. Only since structuralism became a fashion in Paris, in the years after the high tide of existentialism and comparable essentialist modes of thought, did unity of the structuralist approach (its relevance as well as the specificity of the structuralist activity) become clear. This relevance is in accordance with the ideas of Marx, Nietzsche, and Freud, who

— creating a century of fundamental reorientation towards the foundations of Western thought — stressed the plural use rather than the singular self-evidence of the phenomenon *order*. This might be the reason why in contemporary structuralism their texts are continually interpreted and reread. They function as organizing forces within the structuralist discourse of today, the more so as in their texts the structuralist thesis is anticipated. The true philosophical problem is that of *order*, and their texts are to be read as an attempt towards a structuralist activity — the practice of the *plurality of orders* — implying a fundamental relativism.

This process of recognition, presence, and awareness about a set of textual structures functioning in our contemporary society creates a structuralist *milieu*. But, as Anthony Wilden suggests in the preface to his *System and Structure*, the ability to participate in those *milieux* differs widely on both sides of the Channel and the Atlantic Ocean, due to traditional values at work when relevant discourses are constructed. This is clearly the case when one analyses for instance the reception of the works of Lévi-Strauss. In the Anglo-Saxon world critics overlooked the holistic overtones of his *Mythologies,* and they criticized only details of his investigations as well as separate chains of arguments. On the Continent, especially in Paris, no detailed analysis was made, but discussion tended to be polarized: the theory as a whole, including its rather shallow and haphazard philosophical statements, was either taken for granted or rejected. One is a structuralist or one is not. Nevertheless, the gap is still not bridged — not by more general works on the subject, like Wilden's, nor by the fast-increasing number of translations into English, such as the works of Foucault, Barthes, or Althusser.

But in the meantime the structuralist fashion in Paris has faded away and the contemporary situation differs from the time when the German text of this book was written. One could say that structuralism as a Parisian fashion stressed only the first phase in the development of structuralist thought after the Second World War — a development generally based on the main principles of Russian Formalism and Czech literary structuralism. This phase, covering the years 1945-1965/70, i.e. from the first influences of the ideas of Lévi-Strauss and Jakobson until Michel Foucault's *L'ordre du discours*, could be described, in terms of Cubist aesthetic theory, as the analytical phase of structuralism. During this period the connexion between general linguistics and ethnology produced an enormous amount of field research and trans-cultural material, and both aimed at a general theory and at general laws of explanation — not by the construction of a methodological discourse dealing with essentialia but by applying specific procedures like *analysis* and *arrangement*, as well as *differentiation* and *opposition*. These procedures were already applied in the phonology of Troubetzkoy, the linguistic theories of de Saussure and Propp's analyses of literary form. Throughout all the years of the development of the structuralist ideas since the Moscow Circle (1915), Roman Jakobson carried out fundamental and parallel research in these fields. In his works and those of Lévi-Strauss the impression was created that structural linguistics could provide a more or less comprehensive theory, and ethnology the facts of that theory.

The works of Barthes, Foucault, Sollers and Derrida since 1965 developed into a more synthetical phase of structuralism. The idea of a general theory, was shaped to a great extent by the investigation concerning literary theory in particular. Literature was revealed as a process of constant transformation according to laws which are the products of functioning social value-systems. The result of every act of literature as well as of every speechact is a *text*. For that reason a far-reaching identification of the structure of a text and the structure of reality was proclaimed. Even the metaphysical basis of a theory had to be interpreted as a specific textual structure generated by texts, not by individuals. In those textual structures, and nowhere else, sets of speechacts can be produced, So in the synthetic phase of structuralism two intertwining structures play dominant rôles, the structure of texts and the structure of discourses. Although both are *given* — since texts and discourses are never the sole result of a subjective intention — both are at the same time *constructed* — again not by the subjective intention of a scientific observer, but by the values and traditions determining the ensemble and the functioning principles. That is exactly what Michel Foucault once called "anonymous thinking, knowledge without subject, theory without identity."

These ideas lead definitely to new awarenesses concerning the depth-structure of reality. This depth-structure is not exclusively a structure of consciousness but underlies and even constitutes the phenotextual structure of the so-called apparent reality. This again leads to a critical attitude, to creative mistrust (Nietzsche) and relativism. This attitude is closely linked to other problems concerning structures, such as in Chomskian linguistics, in genetics, in biochemistry and cybernetics, in economics, or in social inter-action. This leads to the definite denial of 'a theoretically omniscient observer' (Husserl) and to the promotion of a scientific activity in which the subject's autonomy becomes relative. Human activity is an *inscriptive* activity, and human history has to be seen as an ensemble of *graffiti*.

1974   JAN M. BROEKMAN

CHAPTER I

THE STRUCTURALISTIC ENDEAVOUR

1. THE WORLD AS MUSICAL SCORE

The recent decades of this century have witnessed unusually rapid and far-reaching changes in the use of certain fundamental concepts in art, literature, science, and philosophy. One need do no more than glance at the literary and philosophical journals of this period to form an idea of the extent of this change.

Even before World War II, existential philosophy had been fully developed. Immediately after the war, existentialism reached a fashionable zenith and it became general to speak of the uniqueness of man — of his intrinsic nature, of his historical nature, and of his freedom. Human consciousness, in the philosophical *Gestalt* of a 'subject', obtained as a point of departure in every literary and philosophical endeavour. In prinicple, questions emanating from human consciousness were considered to be amenable to an interpretation that similarly emanated from human consciousness. How productive such extensive hermeneutics were could thus be constantly tested anew. The historical model was taken for granted — descriptive analyses, reaching out even to marginal situations, examined the nature of man as historical concept. Active humanism was an important impetus for every activity that also had a practical objective — the idea of *engagement* was retained as a valuable philosophical and literary concept from the time of the Resistance. Art, literature, and philosophy were part of the same, all-inclusive, evolution. For the world of man was conceived as principally symbolic — the unity of achievement in these fields rested upon the priority given to symbolism. In the same way, the phenomenon of human speech was viewed from the aspect of what it contained.

Meanwhile, a totally different conceptual world developed, which, however — because of circumstances — achieved comparably fashionable expression only at a later stage. It was based on developments, at the turn of the century, in phonology, linguistics, and aesthetics — developments which in turn influenced anthropology and the philosophy of history and politics. Not until the fifties did it become generally recognized as a basic approach in art, science, and philosophy.

This way of thinking challenged the uniqueness and authenticity of man, linked by tradition with the notion that he was, as a creature, self-sufficient. Man perhaps manages occasionally and for a few moments during his life to give off a light of his own; for the rest he must be seen as but an element of a more extensive system. Instead of speaking of the freedom of man, one ought to speak of his being entangled in and fettered to the structure. His consciousness seldom represents the self-sufficiency of his being, but is mostly a product of his being; only then can the self function productively. It is to be taken, not as a condition, but as conditioned.

The problem of interpretation thus lost its courageous and speculative (albeit subjective) fire, being supplanted, instead, by analysis. Analyses of function took the place of the traditional hermeneutics. One no longer dares to pose the question of the essence of man; instead, one focusses attention on his specific function in the context of certain cultures and sub-cultures. The historical model has to a large extent been replaced by a model of the sciences, particularly a theoretical systems model. Humanism has been unmasked as a too ideological approach to philosophy; many Parisian philosophers therefore favour an active anti-humanism, in order that they may not fall victim to all kinds of mystification.

In this sense, the problem of human history is not to be thought of as an evolution, but as a continuing process of transformation. The world in which man is no longer principally historical is a world in which the symbolic is no longer specific; it reveals itself instead as a world of signs. In this context interest in the content of language has lost out to interest in its syntactic and semantic aspects.

In an interview with Madeleine Chapsal in 1966, Michel Foucault, shortly after the publication of his book *Les Mots et les Choses*, which expresses all this in a radical way, retrospectively said:

Suddenly, and without apparent reason, one realised, about fifteen years ago, that one had moved far, very far, away from the previous generation, the generation of Sartre and Merleau-Ponty — the generation of the *Temps Modernes* that used to be the norm for our thinking and the model for our lives. Sartre's generation appeared to us an extremely courageous and magnanimous generation, which passionately invested themselves in life, politics, and existence. We, however — we have discovered something else for ourselves, another passion, the passion for the concept and for that which I would wish to call the system.

The breach became complete when Lévi-Strauss demonstrated for societies and Lacan demonstrated for the unconscious that their 'sense' presumably is nothing but a kind of surface effect, a foam. On the other hand, that which penetrates most deeply into us, that which was there before we were, that which holds us together in time and space — that is indeed the *system*. The 'I' is destroyed (think of modern literature). We are now concerned with the discovery of the 'there is'. We now speak of 'one'. In a certain sense we thus go back to the viewpoint of the seventeenth century, but with the following difference: It is not man we set in the place of God, but anonymous thinking, knowledge without subject, theory without identity.

Foucault, when he made these notes, gathered the tinder with which to fire the debates on structuralism as applied to the traditional themes of philosophy and literature. These now take place particularly by using linguistic concepts, like the contrasts between *langue* and *parole* (language as system and language as the spoken word – a distinction that goes back to de Saussure), between *signifiant* (the indicating) and *signifié* (the indicated), between *code* as element of a language system and *message* as communication or the application of the language, between *synchronie* and *diachronie* (systems approach and historical approach). All these are concepts drawn from a comprehensive 'semiology', a general study of signs .

As structuralism is neither a school of thought nor a movement, neither a philosophical nor a literary current (it is much less any of these than is the afore-mentioned existentialism), one should take note of the regularly repeated use of such terms. Structuralism as a whole is based upon the view that such linguistic concepts, and those related to them, can serve to elucidate not only linguistic problems but also philosophical, literary, and social science problems, as well as problems concerning the theory of science. Moreover, it is only as a result of this way of thinking that an adequate solution to these problems would be achievable.

We thus have to do, not with a point of view based on a given theory of knowledge, but with an intellectual orientation that can be deduced from the current of the argument. We have to do with a concatenation of actions from which the *episteme* must be prepared beforehand, and in which it may in each combination perhaps show a different face. We would thus be consistent in going along with Roland Barthes when he speaks of a structuralistic *activity*, i.e. a regular sequence of a definite number of mental operations only definable by means of their specific terminology. It is indeed only this entirely changed terminology that gives us the feeling of being suddenly aware of living in a world other than that which we have hitherto imagined – in a world, not of individualities, of historical processes, of more-or-less free decisions, of open horizons, but instead in a world of rules, a world seen as a score (Lévi-Strauss), or an array of symbols (Lacan).

It is thus also no wonder that we continue to encounter great disparity in terminology. Every concept that is able to express this view of the universe is acceptable as making structuralistic thought more widely known. With every classical author – whether it be Descartes, Hume, Rousseau, Marx, or Freud – such concepts are to be found. Barthes explains:

The goal of every structuralistic activity, whether reflective or creative, consists of reconstructing an 'object' in such a way that this reconstruction reveals the rules according to which the object functions ... structural man takes what is given or agreed upon, takes it apart, puts it together again; this doesn't seem to be much . . . and yet this moiety, seen from another aspect, is decisive . . . creation or reflexion is not in this case a 'print' of the world that is true to the original, but is a real generation of a world resembling the first, yet setting out not to copy it but to make it explicable. (*4.10*, 191)

This holds in equal measure for the formulae of mathematics as for literary and philosophical texts; as much for psychological theories as for problems of cosmology.

2. THE CONCEPT OF 'STRUCTURE'

In this new structuralistic approach, the chief emphasis obviously falls on the concept 'structure'. Notwithstanding, very few structuralistic thinkers have dealt explicitly with a definition of this concept. They probably considered it to be too controversial. In attaching so little weight to an inductive definition of 'structure', they however are the cause of the first, characteristic, frustration. One might ask whether this frustration is a necessary one. As early as the end of the forties, the American anthropologist Kroeber accorded this concept a central position in his observation, at the same time however criticizing its use, because he foresaw how it might come to be regarded as a rough-and-ready way out of all problems.

'Structure' appears to be just yielding to a word that has a perfectly good meaning but suddenly became fashionably attractive for a decade or so — like 'aerodynamics' — and during its vogue tends to be applied indiscriminately because of the pleasurable connotations of its sound. Of course a typical personality can be viewed as having a structure. But so can a physiology, any organism, all societies and all cultures, crystals, machines — in fact everything that is not wholly amorphous has a structure. (*1.8*, 325).

Nowadays, it would be common purpose that the word 'structure' evokes certain associations on which there is consensus, such as that a structure is a combination of relations, in which the interdependence of parts (elements) is characterized by their relation to the whole (to the totality). This in itself says very little. Structuralism seen as a whole is based on more than merely employing such associations.

Lévi-Strauss repeatedly emphasizes that the structuralistic attempt to discover the 'order' of phenomena does not consist of imposing a preconceived 'order' upon reality. It calls for, instead, reproduction, reconstruction, building a model of that reality. A myth, a philosophical thought, a scientific theory — these not only have a certain content but are also determined by a definite logical organization. This organization indicates antecedents and common elements of such phenomena which otherwise never could have been reduced to a single common denominator. In this way, concepts like 'system' and 'structure' become operational. But the difficulty, signalized by Kroeber and Lévi-Strauss, appears here again: The concept 'structure' either has no sense at all, or its sense already has a structure. The concept of 'structure' is similar to the concept of 'order' in the sense that, should one wish to look up its definition in a dictionary, one becomes aware, in paging the dictionary, that the book itself has a structure, represents an order, thus posing the question whether the definition one will find can be universally valid.

Structures, it appears, do not exist independently from the immediate context of their definition; sociological, cultural-historical, anthropological, or economic definitions of structure cannot inductively lead to a general definition. To renounce an inductive approach, however, opens up wider possibilities, such as a *functional* or a *hypothetico-deductive* approach. The first is either differential or isomorphic; differential in the sense that every element of a structure (and a structure can also function as an element of a more comprehensive totality) is defined by its opposing distinction from all other elements, and isomorphic in the sense that two structures may differ entirely in content but morphologically be identical. Such a functional approach both emphasizes that 'structure' has to be seen in its context and points to the phenomena of synonymy (relatedness in meaning) and homonymy (consonance, but of different meaning).

The functional approach has its roots in that phonology which at the beginning of this century played an important role in Genevan linguistics (de Saussure), and in Russian formalism (Jakobson). A researcher into phonology of language regards sound-elements as meanings — elements, whose meaning however is derived solely from their incorporation into a system. Lévi-Strauss attributes this to the social phenomenon of cognacy. "... the 'systems of cognacy', just as the 'phonological systems', are constructed by the mind on the level of subconscious thinking. The repetition of forms of kinship, rules of marriage, and similarly prescribed associations leads us to suppose that the observed phenomena result, in one case as in the other, from the interplay between general, but hidden, laws. The problem may now be stated as follows: Although they belong to *another order of reality*, kinship phenomena are *of the same type* as linguistic phenomena". (*4.34*, 46) In this functional interpretation, what appeared as inexplicably disconnected now forms part of an order not hitherto foreseeable. Such an order becomes possible only when one takes the seemingly lapidary statement of de Saussure's seriously, viz. that language is a form and not a substance. (*0.22*, 169).

In such structural interpretations as are oriented more towards mathematics than towards phonology, the emphasis shifts to a hypothetico-deductive approach. The notion of structure is then usually linked to a logical construction. The structure of the object is dominated by the logic of the total structure: but, even here, the difficulty remains that the poly-interpretation of 'structure' cannot be avoided. Setting to work in this way is applicable to several widely-differing fields, such as to the factor analysis of Spearman, to Lévi-Strauss's analyses of structure according to kinship systems, to sociometry, or to the sociology of Talcott Parsons.

Even when the structure of a system results from a hypothetico-inductive approach to this system, this theory can assume many distinguishably different logical forms. In one case it may refer to verifiable model-building, in another case to interrelations of verbal propositions that soon tend to become syllogistic, or in a third case it may even refer to verification-units whose criteria (as the analysis proceeds) soon lose their logical character.

In both approaches – the functionalist and the hypothetico-deductive (used without discrimination by most authors on structuralism) – a contradiction remains, this contradiction being between the assumed identity of the concept of structure on the one hand and, on the other, the variety of real relationships that are included in this concept.

As long as such difficulties are not solved, three aspects remain characteristic in the structural use of structure as a concept: polysemantics, contextuality, and permeability.

A. *Polysemy*

For the time being, one cannot get away from the polysemious, or polyvalent, nature of the concept *structure*. One has always to fall back upon an exact analysis of the concept of structure as it was employed in the texts of the relevant author at the time of writing. Thus, for Lévi-Strauss, the concept of structure is used differently in his *Anthropologie Structurale* from the way it is used in his *Mythologiques*: Foucault uses it differently from Barthes. In surveying all the writings on structuralism one is therefore inclined to conclude that what one has on hand is a collection of homologies. In addition, there is the abstruse but nevertheless very close affinity which the concepts *function* and *system* bear to the concept of structure, and also to the scientific procedures based upon them, which may sometimes be described as structural analyses and then again as functional analyses.

Our point of departure is the fact, already established by Carnap, that all scientific statements can be transformed into one statement containing nothing besides structural characteristics plus indications of one or more opposing fields. The structuralistic endeavour, from the point of view of the theory of science, accordingly is a transformation process which sets out to obtain such statements. A structure may be defined as a network of relationships between elements or elementary processes; which concept is more-or-less based upon the possibility of making an instantaneous survey or assessment. A provisional description such as this does not exclude the possibility of the elementary processes referred to above being structurally defined, and of the boundaries of the network of relationships at times being dependent upon the point of view of the observer. Wherever elements nevertheless join to make a whole, structures arise that are put together in a disciplined or orderly way. The resultant whole we call a system — the phenomenon of system-building in an orderly way we call an organization. Viewed from the level of structure, the concept of relationship holds good, while at the level of the organization a new aspect appears, viz. communication. A structure thus manifests itself by means of relationships; a system manifests itself by means of communication of the relevant elements. A function within the system may thus be seen as a communicative relationship. Structural analyses accordingly study the formation of elements and the ways in which their relationships are combined. Functional analyses on the other hand study the products of communication in the system.

Such descriptions of the concept *structure* do not really do away with the difficulties arising from its polysemious nature. In the writings of structuralist authors there is no consensus about what structure actually is. Even if a generally valid concept could be agreed upon, the problem would not be solved. Clarification would still be needed, in the relative context, as to whether the established analogies are for instance based upon a similarity of form or a similarity of function, whether the character of the system and the degree of complexity are in accord, and (if we speak of the object as a system) in which ways structural and systemic factors are complementary. At the same time, a critical question (concerning the structuralistic endeavour seen as a whole) emerges from these uncertainties. Hitherto the systems selected for study have been so complex that, solely for this reason, the above questions (as well as wider-ranging ones arising from the theory of knowledge) could not be discussed on an explicit basis. Epistemological questions, which surely lie at the centre of structuralism, would be elucidated if the object of study were less complex. Instead, we find complexity growing, as involved mythologies and scientific theories are chosen as objects for the structuralistic approach. In the system seen as a whole (i.e. as a structure), spatial, chronological, enduring, and evanescent representations of the order constantly change places with one another. There is as yet no question, in the structuralistic theory of knowledge, of control over such representations.

B. *Contextuality*

All of this is that much more difficult when one bears in mind that *contextuality* plays the most important role in the concept of structure. Indeed, the structuralistic way of thinking may be seriously regarded as an attempt at an *eccentric* way of thinking. One is also reminded of Nietzsche: "Since Copernicus, man rolls out of the centre into an x". (*5.6*,II, 882) The fixed point of departure of every idealistic theory of knowledge — the subject — is abolished; the eccentric manifests itself in the essential contextuality, i.e. in every way of thought that questions itself in so far as it dares to expose itself. The centre of all relationship is no longer predetermined; it changes constantly within the system. As a former part of the system, it itself takes part in the system. Here too linguistics has contributed to our awareness — no single element of a system can be defined except via its opposite relationship to all other elements — this holds even for the element by which the system is recognized, which is the token of the whole.

In this connexion, Boudon distinguishes two types of context (*1.4*, 35ff) — one in which the concept of structure is employed *intentionally* (and in which it thus plays a preponderantly significative role), and the other a context in which the concept is used *effectively* and in which it plays a role that is mainly constructive.

Examples of intentional use are to be found in philosophy, sociology, *Gestalt* psychology, etc. The reader is reminded of Gurvitch's distinction between structured and non-structured groups, of Carnap's notion of a logical construct of the world, of Goldstein's composition of an organism, and of Merleau-Ponty's analysis of the structure of corporeality. Structure is here regarded, not for its own sake, but in connexion with the group, the organism, the world, and corporeality. The logical form of such a use of the concept of structure is predominantly distinctive. The contextuality is necessary solely to make the distinction possible.

When Gurvitch's or Merleau-Ponty's analyses are compared with those of Lévi-Strauss or Chomsky, it becomes apparent that in the latter more effective use is made of the interconnexions between structure and context. The question arises, in scientific theories of structure, whether structure is a goal in itself or whether individual objects may also be designated according to structural attributes. Object, structure, and context are settled by one another reciprocally. The object can only be understood from the totality of the organization, whereas the organization itself is determined by the object system. The recourse to system theory (von Bertalanffy) is to be understood in this sense; the system characteristics of the object are prerequisites for the structuralistic conceptualization of the object. (*1.3*)

The latter point emerges very clearly from descriptions of structure when they are of a non-scientific or a non-epistemological nature. To illustrate, a fragment is chosen from the Codex Florentius (*0.2*, 8). The eccentric position of the characteristic subject within the system of definition is here clearly shown. "ABYSS — there it is deep. It is a difficult, dangerous place, a deadly place. There it is dark, there it is light. It is an abyss."

C. *Permeability*

The foregoing has already illustrated the permeability of the concept of structure. At the present stage, it is virtually impossible to get away from its multiplicity. The context plays an important role because every element, when the structure is created, in principle counts for the same. In structuralism, scientific and non-scientific descriptions of structure constantly interchange. Various approaches function indistinguishably — philosopho-epistemological, literary, aesthetic, political, et al. Permeability refers to the relativity of content, and to the prior position accorded to what is formal and relational. Roland Barthes describes structuralism as follows: "As structuralism is neither a school nor a movement, there is no reason a *priori* to restrict it to scientific thought. One ought rather to try to describe (if not to define) it as broadly as possible on a level different from that of reflective language. It in any case stands to reason that there are writers, painters, and musicians in whose eyes the *bringing* of structure *into practice* (not only thinking about structure) represents a distinctive experience. It also stands to reason that one must include analytic as well as creative activity under the same common head. What may be termed *structural man* is not he who is defined via his ideas or his language but via his imagination, or, preferably, via *what he imagines* — thus via the way in which he mentally experiences the structure. Accordingly, structuralism is, for *all* who are able to make use of it, in essence an occupation ..." (*4.10*, 191).

In summary, one can describe this new occupation, this endeavour, as a process whereby one becomes aware of certain methodological principles. We thus do not have to do with a new literature, aesthetics, philosophy, or science; neither do we have to do with a new method seeking to oust all previous methods in the human sciences. Structuralist insight may be traced back to two important sources of inspiration. Linguistically its source is de Saussure; mathematically its source is that polycephalic genius we know by the name of Bourbaki. De Saussure contributed to the insight that language seen as a system is an equally important theme of linguistics as it previously was a theme of the history of language. Just as no single element of a language system can be determined without its relationships to all other elements of the same system, so, according to the conceptualization inspired by these insights, every experience is reduceable to a system of correlative elements. Bourbaki at first conceived of mathematics as a study of structure. i.e. of systems of the relationships between elements. The characteristics of these elements do not exist on their own; they can only be deduced from the framework of their relationships.

Meanings are thus relatively stated in terms of relationships. The construction (or in other words the technique) is recognized as the essence of every human act of creation; the object is each time put together anew to allow functions to become apparent. The method as revealed by the work is often more important than the work that the method brought into being.

Structuralism as endeavour is accordingly based upon practices and insights — not upon a genuine methodological theory. The 'reading' of facts is not confined merely to a 'reading off' of facts from the concatenation of all that which is given. The 'reading' will have to develop itself with the aid of theoretical models — models that not only assist theory-building, but actually provide approaches to the structures of reality. In this sense, Lévi-Strauss correctly emphasizes that the structure itself will have to be *constructed*. In stating this as an expectation he aligns himself with von Neumann's and Morgenstern's *Theory of Games* (1944):

Such models are theoretical constructs with a precise, exhaustive and not too complicated definition; and they must be similar to reality in those respects which are essential in the investigation at hand .... Similarity to reality is needed to make the operation significant.

3. EPISTEMOLOGICAL GROUNDS

The lack of a genuine theory of method does not mean that no important views on structuralism emerge from epistemology.

The first of these important views is closely related to that set out above. Science can only exist if it keeps away from the immediacy of experience in general. The bond with immediacy is an obstacle in any effort to grasp the generic.

The second important point of departure in structuralism is linked with this. What has been said above does not necessarily have to lead to a strictly rationalistic interpretation. Quite the contrary. Most authors substitute a more comprehensive holistic approach for a primarily rationalist approach. Structuralism may thus be reckoned among those modern scientific approaches which, without disparaging or underrating what is rational, nevertheless espouse the irrational, viewed scientifically. In this way, a similarity becomes apparent with Wittgenstein's formulations concerning the mystical — formulations which have been overlooked only by the dogmatic logico-positivists. The *Tractatus Logico-Philosophicus*, 6.44, states: "The mystical is not *how* the world is, but the fact *that* it is". 6.522: "There is, of course, the inexpressible. This manifests itself, it is the mystical." The same goes for man. Lévi-Strauss speaks of the end of the golden era of the awareness of history, of a world that began without man and that will also come to an end without him (*4.33, 3.74*). Similarly, Foucault sees man as an invention that dates back barely two centuries, an irregularity in our *generic* knowledge finds a new form (*4.51,* 15).

From all of this emerges a third important approach based on the theory of knowledge — a relativism based on a new principle. It had its origins in the essential relativism of cultural anthropology and of linguistics on an ethno-linguistic basis. If one sets out to make a thorough study of the systematic nature of the different languages and especially of their indicative systems, one has to acknowledge the parity, the co-equality, of them all. A chance is thus created to place Western culture comparatively beside anthropocentrism. As every linguistic researcher personally experienced at the beginning of the present century, this process did not escape ideological and political consequences. What has been quoted here from Lévi-Strauss and Foucault reflects the same relativism. The practice of structuralism will, looked at in this way, always at the same time imply the practice of relativism. The connexions between the theory of knowledge and structuralism, inspired by phonology and mathematics, constitute a further step towards the relativist reflexions of Nietzsche or Wittgenstein and their radical equating of philosophy and linguistic criticism. It also constitutes a further step beyond the metalinguistics of a writer such as Whorf, whose relativism is clarified by using the concept of structure, with its contextuality, permeability, and its capacity to be formalized.

The fourth approach — the farewell to philosophical idealism — fits in with the foregoing insofar as the rôle of the subject is central to the discussion. Foucault writes about the destruction of the 'I', and focusses interest on the 'there is'. In doing so, he attacks the idealistic priority accorded to the philosophizing, self-ruling, self-sufficient subject and discloses it as a linguistic custom of our Western culture that masks reality. The 'I', the subject, is neither the centre of itself, nor the centre of the world — it is only that, thus far, it has taken itself to be these. Such a centre does not exist at all. Foucault, Althusser, Lacan — they all start their thinking with a *décentrement* of the subject. Every centre is a functional element of the system; the system does not *have* a centre, it *creates* centres *for itself,* at will and in accordance with and its changing needs. Seen in this perspective, humanism, too, is an idealistic fallacy; one that has reduced dignity to an ideological trick. To liberate oneself from this humanism is — as Althusser shows — at the same time a political act, implying the denial of any philosophical anthropology.

We have, however, to be very careful here and should not draw premature conclusions. Neither history nor what is human, neither the subject nor the 'I', nor anthropology, are being denied in an absolute sense; such absolute denial would be contrary to the relativism of structuralist thinking. We have only just begun to draw conclusions from our insight into the limitations of the traditional views on the 'content' aspects of human existence, and into the consequences that follow when we turn instead to looking at the 'form' aspects of this existence. Barthes says:

Structuralism does not deprive the world of history: it tries to commit history not only to content (that has been done a thousand times over), but also to form; not only to the material, but also to the intelligible; not to the ideological, but also to the aesthetic. Precisely because every thought about what is historically intelligible is in itself a contribution to the intelligible, it doesn't matter to structural man whether he will turn out to be lasting. He knows that structuralism, too, is a specific *form* of the world which will change with the world, Just as he sees his validity (not his truth) as lying in the capacity to speak old languages in a new way, he also knows that his task has come to an end as soon as a new language appears in history, which then speaks to *him*. (*4.10*, 196)

As has been said: Structuralism in practice is the practice of *this* (and no other) relativism.

4. SOCIOLOGY AND STRUCTURALISM

On the one hand, we have a structuralist sociology whose problem above all lies in its relation to functionalism. On the other hand we have a sociological approach to structuralism.

A. *Structuralism and Functionalism*

A sociology influenced by structuralism is in the first place linked to relativism. It gives high priority to a comparative study of social structures, and concerns itself with the problem of the antitheses represented by nature and culture, and the interplay between them. This is done with particular reference to ethnology, cultural anthropology, the sociology of language, and ethnolinguistics. The researches of Durkheim, Mauss, Boas, Kroeber, Lowie, Malinowski, and Radcliffe-Brown should be especially mentioned here. Lévi-Strauss, incumbent of the Chair of Sociology at Sao Paulo, Brazil from 1935-

1939, also belongs to this list. The point of departure for all these writers was not sociological and ethnological intuition about 'the' social structure, 'the' meaning of social life, 'the' culture, but rather their own concrete re-searches into the ramifications of specific social structures. So-doing, Lévi-Strauss penetrates deeply into philosophical dimensions – he is well-acquain-ted with the realms of thought of Rousseau, Marx, and Freud (*4.42*). – and turns in reports of high literary quality (*Tristes Tropiques*) without setting out to be philosopher or *littérateur*. Time and again experience illustrates to the cultural anthropologist that he is inclined to see cultures where changes are not rapid as forerunners of our own Western concepts and ways of life. Yet time and again the truth turns out to be otherwise – this gives rise in Lévi-Strauss case to a certain nostalgia.

Two examples are taken here from Lévi-Strauss's descriptions. The Bororo, a tribe in Central Brazil, manifest a view of the world and of life that might be equated to the more differentiated thinking of the West. Central to this view is the problem of death. When a man dies, say the Bororo, this not only affects his next of kin, but affects the whole social structure. Death may be *natural*, but it is at the same time *anti-cultural*. Should nature permit harm to come to society through a death, the least that can be done is to kill and bury a jaguar so as to restore the equilibrium, the order. Thus man is buried twice.

Another example: Caduevo Indians paint their faces in *geometrical* de-signs. They do this in order to emphasize the dignity of man – to stress his transition from nature to culture, which is a self-conscious transition, not to be interpreted symbolically. These Indians go about in nature as living sym-bols of membership of their culture.

To such sociological analyses must be added others not so immediately inspired by ethnology. We think for instance of Lucien Goldmann's analy-ses of the sociology of literature; of Roland Barthes's analyses of the fashion, myths, and images of our industrial society; or of Louis Althusser's interpre-tations of Marxism. Urs Jaeggi (*1.6*) has further information to give us about these contributions. Thus far we have, however, not yet seen a thematically analysed, comprehensive, and consistent work on structuralist sociology.

Goldmann's critique of an a-historical sociology (*4.4, 4.5*) illustrates how closely the work of structuralists in the field of sociology approaches Mer-ton's analyses of norms, or the functionalism of Talcott Parsons. The inter-mingling of social structure and social function Goldmann interprets as the driving motor of history. That is to say, the anthropological theme which we may call 'the historical nature of man' lies in the intertwining of social structure and social function. Insofar as structuralist thinking leads to the separation of structure from function, it destroys this essential historical character. Goldmann merely points to the possibility of this danger; whether it in fact exists remains an open question which should be precisely inquired into in the future.

When structuralism is strictly and formally employed, the above-mentioned separation, with all its consequences, will ensue. By strict and formal structuralism is meant an orientation directed solely to examining the most general thought structures — structures thus that are to be found in all societal forms, and which (thanks to the way the models are constructed) are not subject to historical change. One has anew to remind oneself that such an approach is only possible via the construction of models, but that by constructing models one is not making any pronouncement upon the extent to which social reality is based on fact. Lévi-Strauss, for example, has always underlined this. The other side of this approach produces sociological functionalism. Here one encounters a network of acutely topical problems, ranging from Parsons on the one hand to the controversies about positivism in sociology on the other. Goldmann sees functionalism as being conservative in that it evokes interest only in the stabilizing forces in every institution within the given society. According to him, the 'functional' aspect does not really touch upon the problem of change; analyses of the 'dysfunctional' never get away from the cadre of the functional. Thus the possibilities of real innovation are excluded. This problem is shared by an a-genetic structuralism.

Here, too, terminological errors and confusions are to be found. The distinction between structure and function has not been clearly worked out and the dynamism of the functional, with its contextuality and permeability, has been left out of account. One is inclined to suspect that with the term 'genetic structuralism' an historical concept, idealistic in origin, is once again being introduced. From a methodological point of view, there can be no objection to leaving the diachronic, genetic aspect temporarily out of consideration. But Goldmann's criticism is valuable insofar as it shows that the synchronic nature of the structuralist conception may cause the diachronic to be lost sight of.

B. *Towards a Sociology of Structuralism*

In establishing a sociology of structuralism, the efforts of Jean Améry and François Furet were particularly important — in what they did they limited themselves to French structuralism. Schiwy's work on the subject is based on their statements (*1.1, 1.5, 0.12*). The principal thesis of this sociological interpretation of structuralism is that structuralism should be seen as a philosophy of frustrated French leftist intellectuals. Nihilism is a constant companion to this frustration and finds excellent expression in the main thought of the structuralists. This main thought is reduced to three themes: the denial of history, the denial of the subject, and a denial of the individual and pessimistic view of the future of Western society, as developed by Lévi-Strauss, Foucault, Barthes, and others. The outcome of these structuralist trains of thought may be inferred from the attitude of the structuralists towards Marxism, from their interpretation of an ideology of the non-ideological, and from their endorsement of the present-day universal technocracy.

Améry concentrates upon the structuralist conception of history. The frustration of leftist intellectuals, he says, is clearly to be deduced from the evasion, in their thinking, of topical involvement; from their retreat from the revolution that hasn't taken, and (after 1945) probably will not take, place; and the disgust they display towards the historical. The fact that France's role as a great power in the history and politics of the world now definitely seems to be played out, is in addition a cardinal theme.

In other words, this frustration is reputed to be the negative result of the undoubtedly relativist elements that the work of Lévi-Strauss and other structuralists contains. But the analysis goes no further than the rejection of a certain Europe-centred and nationalist conception of history. It does not seek to inquire whether rejecting this conception of history does not open up positive possibilities. On the contrary, the sociological analysis tries to bring yet more negative elements of the structural view to the fore, so that the averred frustration may appear more plausible. The anti-humanism of Althusser or Foucault, the denial of a humanist philosophical anthropology in the later works of Marx, and other structuralist themes all serve to highlight the truism that the subject, when it no longer involves itself, is powerless. Moreover, Améry and Furet show that structuralism will have robbed the West of every trace of missionary consciousness, seeing that the loss of Europe- and anthropocentrism has in practice become so evident in everyday life. Schiwy adds to this by saying that this conclusion must be regarded as final, because European intellectuals apparently have landed in an ideological vacuum, from out of which structuralism just does not point the way.

Negativism evoked in this way is, however, very one-sided. This becomes immediately apparent when one bears in mind that such analyses are founded upon the destinies of one specific stratum of one specific nation. The development of structuralism is far from being exclusively French and postwar. It goes back to the Russian formalism of the beginning of our century, and has in many respects determined the intellectual climate of Europe. Groups of intellectuals were then already discussing aesthetic and political problems (as well as ethno-linguistic, mathematical, and phonological ones) in formalist terms — intellectuals who could in no sense be classified into political categories as crude as 'left' or 'right', but who nevertheless demonstrated by their actions that they were in oppositon, i.e. that they were anti-dogmatic, or relativist. The political destinies of Europe forced them to put relativism into practice. This practice sometimes led them to the brink of nihilism, as may be inferred from the often despairing discussions of dogmatic Marxism and Stalinism, dogmas that were increasingly regarded as stifling. Barely ten years after the Russian revolution, emigration was the only way out one could take. The famous 'Prague Circle' was an expatriate continuation of the Moscow cirlce of linguists. The next decade saw emigration to other centres — first the *Lingvistkreis* offered a haven in Copenhagen, thereafter the 'Linguistic Circle of New York'. Améry's statement — that Lévi-Strauss supplies a systematic philosophy for an area that no longer knows what it is like to expect revolution — should, however, be regarded as a gross oversimplification and a foreshortening of historical perspectives. Lévi-Strauss does not supply a philosophy, and particularly not at all a systematic one. Revolutionary experiences, such as associated with the Russian revolution and the rise of Hitler's *Reich*, have constantly been linked with the growth of structuralist thinking. But they have led neither to a humanistic philosophy nor to a nihilist one.

Comparing the state of structuralism before World War II with its French period after that war, one observes tendencies that are to a certain extent contradictory. Formalist and structuralist intellectuals before the war focussed on opposition; they were anti-dogmatic and non-nationalistic in their thinking, which was also strongly relativist. But the second generation indeed largely did lose its oppositional and, particularly, its anti-dogmatic character. Relativism in turn transformed itself into nihilism. Does this, however, hold also for those who today would be counted among the structuralist thinkers? One might be able to accuse Althusser in this way, to a lesser extent Foucault, but certainly not Lévi-Strauss. Sociological analysis must therefore tread carefully — it must distinguish between structuralist thinkers who have real philosophical, literary, or political significance and those 'structuralists' to whom this approach is merely a matter of fashion, of which nobody can foretell how long it will last. This distinction, deep as an abyss, was also discernible between the existentialists of St. Germain des Prés and the philosophers described, for instance, by Simone de Beauvoir in *Les Mandarins*.

The social psychology components of structuralism as a phenomenon of fashion, including the social dynamics of the Paris Circle and the activities of publishers and editors of the periodicals on the *rive gauche*, would accordingly be more interesting than the expositions of Améry and Furet. The former have at least *created* a fashion out of structuralism: the phenomenon, that in our mass-media society such fashions are indeed created, has great relevance. The writings of Lévi-Strauss, for instance, became generally known only after, in 1958, the book *Anthropologie Structurale* was collated — not written. Because the contents had been *written* earlier — the earliest essay in the book was published as early as 1944 - 1945, the most recent essay in the book dates from 1954. All chapters had at least once already appeared in print elsewhere. The same goes for Jacques Lacan's *Écrits* (1966), a collection of essays written over the years 1937 - 1966. When issued, there was not a single new word in it. But these two books were bought, were successful, came into fashion — without, however, being thoroughly read. Such sociologically relevant facts, themselves prompting deeper study, were studied neither by Améry, nor Furet, nor by others.

Seen from the philosophical point of view and in connexion with Améry's observations, it should be noted that nihilism (also dealt with in sociological analyses) remained an imperfectly understood relativism. Apparently the same holds here. Whether certain European intellectual circles have been fascinated by a latent nihilism, as has been suggested by sociological analysis, is one question. Whether this phenomenon is at all relevant for structuralism, is another. Even if both were true, it still does not tell us all there is to know about nihilism as a significant philosophical concept. All branches of relativism known on structuralism therefore by no means produce the *same* kind of nihilism in each of the many widely differing structuralistic *milieux*.

Nietzsche has described the relationship between nihilism and relativism in a penetrating and satirical way: "There are many eyes. The sphinx, too, has eyes — and consequently there are many 'truths', and consequently there is no truth". (*5.6*, III, 844) Among the texts that may be considered closely akin to the structuralistic *Pensée Sauvage* (*1, 42*) are, interestingly enough, those of Nietzsche — or for the French may be those of Antoine de Saint-Exupéry. The practice of structuralist thinking, as stimulated by the works of Lévi-Strauss, could be very well explained with the aid of some categories from Nietzsche's philosophy. Nietzsche for instance speaks of an "exhibition of cultural and intellectual history". Structuralism marks the "end of the old confidence". It brings about the "self-suspension of Western morals and ideals of truth". This practice draws life from a new "consciousness of history" which no longer recognizes an *a priori* sense in history but instead places man in the central position of him who creates the meaning. Understood this way, structuralist thinking gives rise to Nietzsche's demand for "post-nihilist values". Nihilism is both self-evident and necessary if such values are to be discovered. But the values will nevertheless remain hidden to all those who cannot go beyond a nihilism that is so narrowly conceived.

For Lévi-Strauss, Nietzsche's saying that "real man is of much greater value than man *desired* according to any ideal hitherto" (*5.6*,III, 675) would certainly be valid. "We do not know nearly enough to be able to measure the value of our actions: above all we lack the possibility of taking an objective view: even when we reject an action, we are not judges, but *ex parte...*" (*5.6*,III, 294). This must be understood as an attempt to put nihilistic values into practice in our Western culture. Those for whom structuralism is no more than a fashion would not appreciate this. The others respond to a new consciousness of history, in which, from out of the ashes of a nationalistic and Europe-centred picture of history, rises the vision of man as a creator of meaning. In addition, an effort is being made to design a philosophy which does not turn *against* technics in a way that is romantically and pessimistically critical of the culture, but tries instead to understand and accept technics. As Foucault says: "The endeavour at present undertaken by some of our generation does not consist in standing up for man against science and technique, but of demonstrating clearly that our thinking, our lives, our way of being, right down to the details of our day-to-day behaviour, are all part and parcel of one and the same organizational scheme. Consequently, they depend on the same categories as do the scientific and technical universe. It is the 'human heart' that is abstract. We, however, set ourselves the task of establishing a relationship between man and his science, his discoveries, and his world, which is a concrete world". (*0.8, 94*)

CHAPTER II

MOSCOW

Moscow and St. Petersburg, Prague, Paris: three stations along the route taken in the development of structuralist thought. The actual word 'structuralism', however, did not appear until later; that is, not until the occasion when, in Prague in 1935, The Prague Circle met to distinguish its activities from earlier Russian formalism, and to focus clearer attention on the basic concept of 'structure'. The limits, within which the cultural-historical continuum of structuralist thought is set, coincide chronologically with the present century, and spatially with the European cities mentioned above.

The roots of structuralist thought are to be found in Russian formalism. This important current in Russian intellectual life during the twenties chiefly involves a specific literary and aesthetic theory, according to which neither the artist's biography, nor political or philosophical aspects of his world, nor psychological or sociological factors can adequately explain his literary work. The autonomy of such a work precludes extra-literary justification: if it is to be analysed, therefore, this can only be done on literary grounds, or according to the theory of literature.

1. CONSTELLATIONS

A. *Circles*

The formalist approach links with the school of linguistics developed in Geneva, particularly with statements of Ferdinand de Saussure, and with the initial developments of phonology (Baudouin de Courtenay). These new ideas had a considerable influence on aesthetico-literary thinking, not only *ex* Geneva, but also *via* Moscow and Petersburg. The central figure in such streams of thought was Roman Jakobson, born in Moscow in 1896, leader of the Moscow Circle of Linguists (1915), theorist in Russian futurism (*Futurizm*, 1919; *Novejsaja russkaja poézija*, 1921) and, under the pseudonym Aljagrov, the poet of the 'Transmental Book', *Zaumnaja Kniga*, 1918.

After Jakobson had moved to Czechoslovakia in 1920 a book appeared in Russian, written by Gorky, printed in Berlin, and entitled: *Czech and Russian Verse Compared.* It contained the first analysis of poetry that was phonological, not phonetic — an analysis, that is, of differences in meaning according to differences in sound. Jakobson said of this in 1966: "Functional phonology: it grasps the relationship between sound and meaning. I was influenced by the early works of Sechehaye, the important pupil of de Saussure. What today would, following Martinet, be described as 'double articulation' is already described there. I spoke of two 'layers' — the phonological layer (that of the units which differentiate the meaning without containing the meaning, i.e. the phonemes) and the grammatical layer". (0.8, 48)

In March 1925, exactly ten years after the founding of Moscow's linguistic Circle, plans for founding a similar Circle in Prague were laid. The Prague linguist Mathesius, as well as Trnka, Karčevsky, and Jakobson, were among the planners, and on 16 October 1928 the Prague Circle came into being. From here, first formalist and later structuralist ideas were to influence European linguistics. Linguistics, aesthetics, and literary theory, together with basic philosophical problems associated with them, became themes for discussion. In 1935, both Husserl and Carnap addressed the Circle. Jakobson and Tynjanov, in 1928, in an article in the journal *Nowy Lef* entitled 'Problems in Literary and Linguistic Research', provide us with a summary of formalism and a programme of structuralist research. When the First Congress for Slavistics was held in Prague in 1929, the 'theses' of the Prague Circle, later to become well-known, were formulated. Further Circles of linguistics followed — in 1931 in Copenhagen and in 1934 in New York. Both later provided asylum for linguists forced into exile by the outbreak of the Second World War.

The Parisian periodical *Tel Quel* recently published an essay by Roman Jakobson marking the fiftieth anniversary of the Moscow Linguistic Circle. This may be regarded as the final component of the overview of the formalist-structuralist movement as here outlined. This article advocates that understanding of literature be based solely on a certain autonomy of the text. The text presents the poet's unalienable material; it is an independent structure, whose values do not depend upon extra-linguistic information. It is no coincidence that a French translation (by T. Todorov) rendered many of the basic texts of Russian formalists more accessible, and that its introduction was written by Roman Jakobson. It appeared in 1966 in Paris, in a series running parallel to the periodical *Tel Quel*. The literary theory it presents links up with many works associated with Parisian structuralism, such as: *De la grammatologie*, 1967, by Jacques Derrida; *Semiotike: Recherches pour une sémanalyse*, 1969, by Julia Kristeva; and the collection *Théorie d'ensemble*, 1968. Understandably, these works encourage debate with the phonology and linguistics of Baudouin de Courtenay, de Saussure, Jakobson, Hjelmslev, Bloomfield, and Chomsky.

Moscow and St. Petersburg are the birthplaces of the formalist movement. Victor Erlich, in his monograph *Russian Formalism*, 1955, gives us useful information. So does Jurij-Striedter, in the introductory chapter, 'Zur formalistischen Theorie der Prosa und der literarischen Evolution', of his edition of *Texte der Russischen Formalisten*, 1969. The works of Dimitry Tschiževsky are also relevant. Lévi-Strauss devoted an essay 'La structure et la forme', 1960, to the relation between formalism and structuralism.

One of the most important characteristics of the formalist movement is its own specific form of organization. This form, deeply rooted in Russian intellectual life, may nowadays be rediscovered in Paris Circles. Jakobson narrates how, as long ago as the beginning of the nineteenth century, various circles prospered in Russia, called *krug, kruzok* (diminutive), or *kruzki* (plural). Koenig, in his book *Literarische Bilder aus Russland*, 1837, reports upon them, saying: "German philosophy became known far earlier in Russia than in France and England, where even now real understanding is lacking. (This holds especially for German idealism.) "But the young generation not only differs from the older where the spread of German taste and German lines of thought are concerned; it seeks far more, viz. a deeper understanding, a philosophical penetration, into the manifestation of the German spirit".

Symbolism, futurism, and other aesthetic movements were also connected with the *kruzki*. In their monograph *Literaturnye kruzki i salony*, 1929, Aronson and Rejser describe the fortunes of these circles until the time when Marxism's torpidity and dogmatism put an end to their tradition. The Moscow Circle, *Moskovskij Lingvisticeskij Kruzok* 1925, counted among its seven founder members Roman Jakobson, Bogatyrew (afterwards an authority on Slavic ethnology), Jakovlev, and Buslaev. Vinokor joined later. Brik and Tomasěvsky co-operated closely, and Pasternak and Mandelstam joined. Majakovskij read many of his literary works, and was often invited to discussions. A lively and *avant garde* literary activity developed, the details of which, regrettably, are now however lost. A monograph on this and on the Petersburg Circle would be very important for deeper understanding of the formalist and structuralist movement.

The Moscovites of course had good relations with the Petersburg Circle, whose members later arrived at a consistent aesthetic and literary theory: the *Opojaz*. This is the theory of the 'Petersburg Society for the Study of Poetical Language', founded in 1916/1917 on the initiative of Brik, its main representatives being Sklovsky, Eichenbaum, and Bernstein. Some of the Opojaz members, like Jakubinsky and Polivanov, were interested in linguistic problems; whereas others, particularly under the influence of Russian futurism, concerned themselves with questions in the theory of literature.

Eichenbaum and Sklovsky belonged to the latter. Here, too, Majakovsky often was a stimulating guest. Sklovsky in particular played a leading part, the more so since a brief apprenticeship to a sculptor and good connexions with futurist poets had given him experiences which were to prove fruitful to him when constructing his theory. "With the aid of futurism and modern sculpture one was already able to understand much. At that time I learned to understand art as an independent system". So wrote Sklovsky in his auto-biography: *The Third Factory*. The same goes for Jakobson. As he said in 1966 in an interview with Faye: "Artists and not scholars influenced me most: Picasso, Braque, Chlebnikov, Joyce, Stravinsky. From 1913 to 1914 I lived among painters; I was a friend of Malevic's. He wanted me to go to Paris with him".

B. *The Intellectual Climate*

The history of the origin and development of Russian formalism is charac-terized by a diversified intellectual climate. Influence can be traced from the Geneva school of linguistics (especially from de Saussure, and, *via* him, also from the phonology of the Polish linguist Baudouin de Courtenay), from Husserl's phenomenology (more particularly from the *Logische Untersuchungen*, II, 1901), and also from symbolism, futurism, and cubism.

In the years 1906 to 1911, Ferdinand de Saussure delivered three series of lectures in Geneva on Indo-European languages. In line with tradition, he did so in the first place by means of a description of the history of those languages. Nevertheless, in these lectures the idea was mooted that the history of a language could also be thought of as a sequence of elements within an interacting system. Thus, in opposition to the linguistic tradition, interest in one single language, in its composition, and in its organization, grew. Af-ter de Saussure's death in 1915, the *Cours de linguistique générale* was colla-ted, a book that may well be counted among the most influential linguistic works of this century. It presents two perspectives, both modern and philoso-phically relevant. The first of these is that linguistics is an embedded part of a general study of symbols or signs. In the second, a fundamental scheme, going back to John Locke, is revised, according to which words are signs for 'ideas in the mind', whereas images themselves are signs for objects in the world outside the mind that are 'meant' by words.

According to de Saussure, grammar is the oldest 'science' of language. Philology develops next, and is historically oriented. Still later, with the work of Franz Bopp (*Konjugationssystem der Sanskritsprachen*, 1816), compara-tive linguistics develops. De Saussure's own position is to be gauged from the fact that he distinguishes linguistics from philology, and the science of language from the science of speech. His pair of concepts *langue* and *parole* serve this purpose. *Parole* refers to the individual moment in my speaking, and thus indicates how the language is used. *Langue* on the other hand refers to the language itself as a social system of signals and sounds, in which I might be able to express myself. The relationship between the two is accepted by modern research as the fundamental antithesis between competence in language *(langue)* and the way language is used. In addition, we have the concept of *faculté de langage*, which refers to the general human capacity to be able to speak some or other 'natural' language.

Peripheral to these problems we not only find questions from the field of developmental psychology, but also relevant philosophical questions about the conditions in which a language is experienced, and, in a more general context, about the relationship between language and thought.

We have already seen that the contrast between synchrony and diachrony continues to play an important role in present-day structuralist vocabulary. This terminology, too, goes back to de Saussure; in every linguistic observation, he shifts the main emphasis from the diachronical aspect to the synchronical aspect. There are other ways of understanding a language than by tracing its evolution, or viewing it as a composition of linguistic elements (as in particular etymology does). One probably understands a language much better, and above all understands the essence of verbal communication better, when one places more emphasis on the relations between linguistic elements at one and the same time; i.e. when one pays special attention to the synchrony of the language.

Related to this, furthermore, is the concept of language as a system of signs. This concept has deeply influenced formalism, and probably also structuralism. According to de Saussure, a language sign is a link between a concept and an acoustic image. Signs do not represent other realities. They are arbitrary, which means that they are realities in themselves. This brings us to Michel Foucault's main theme in *Les mots et les choses,* 1966. Signs have a value of their own, and they always relate to one another. If there were no such relationship at all, there would no longer be signs. Their distinctiveness as signs only exists within the network of their relationships.

In any system of signs, two components have always to be distinguished: *le signifiant* (that which is meant) and *le signifié* (content). The relationship between the two constitutes the nucleus of the sign. This does not make sense, however, unless one at the same time remembers that language signs are essentially conventional; they are not a gift of Nature. They share this fundamental conventionality with other systems of signs (e.g. with traffic

signs). This is why, in post-Saussurian linguistics, and above all in sturctura-
lism, so much importance is attached to the idea of a general semiotics (or
science of signs).

Moreover, such approaches made it possible for phonological and basic
mathematical research to become of great importance in linguistics. In
this way, the separation between linguistics and the theory of literature
had, in a few decades, taken a new orientation which could not yet have been
foreseen when de Saussure gave his lecture series in Geneva. These principles
were in any case to retain their paramount position until Chomsky's *Syntactic Structures* appeared in 1957. They dominated formalist thinking, as, in
the beginning, they also dominated structuralist thinking. The reverse was,
however, also true: the widespread influence of formalism created an intellectual climate in which such principles could be accepted and elaborated.

From all of this we may conclude that Russian formalism initially was a
literary and aesthetic movement. The structural approach thus did not spring
directly from mathematical or philosophical considerations but primarily
from aesthetics. This may also be seen from other influences upon the formalist movement, such as symbolism, futurism, and phenomenology.

Neo-Kantianism, Nietzsche, the philosophy of life, and Oscar Wilde – these
were among the themes discussed at the famous Wednesday evening gather-
ings in the tower of Vjaceslac Ivanov at St. Petersburg in the years 1905 to
1910. Russian symbolism mainly developed here, and it was its philosophical
content that distinguished it from French symbolism. Verlaine or Mallarmé
may have been looking for a new way of poetical expression, but Russian
symbolism sought a new interpretation of the totality, maybe a new ontology. Symbolistic literature itself was meant, by means of new ways of expression, to give rise to a new interpretation of existence. Erlich tries to explain
this need in his previously-mentioned monograph. He sees symbolism as the
last effort of a bourgeois aesthetics to maintain itself against the force of an
on-coming, all-pervading revolution.

From a literary point of view, symbolism implies that distinctions between
form and content, the symbol and the symbolized, sound and meaning, must
be stated relatively because they are all aspects of one and the same organic
structure – that of real poetry, of the real work of art. For this reason, we
find among the Russian symbolists a system of signs with a minimum of
relationships that are be to rationally understood, but a maximum of fascina-
tion. The consequence of this is important: it has an effect of alienation,
which one actually finds in all of Russian literature, even among the formalists, who thought of themselves as opposing the symbolists. The 'fascinative'
use of language opens up perspectives, and makes symbols and ways of

presentation possible, which bring about multiple interpretations of a work of art. In this very way, the work of art is imbued with aesthetic value.

Futurism may in part be seen as a reaction to such symbolism, but here, too, alienation plays an important rôle. Majakovsky criticises the role of the human mind in symbolistic aesthetics. Overrating of the ideas of totality and organicity implies that the function of the mind is reduced to passivity and receptivity, and its constructive capacity is thus denied. This inevitably gives rise to an unscientific view of literary reality, leading us back to an idealistic aesthetics in which organistic imitation is regarded as the basics of all art. Art, according to futuristic concepts, is not a copy of Nature, but the preparedness to distort Nature, within the individual mind, according to Nature's reflexions. Two philosophically relevant dual aspects have to be noted here. First, one re-encounters the phenomenon of alienation, implicit in the willingness to distort. Second, a basic attitude, scientific and positive, may be found to be present, especially in the constructive aspects of the activities of the human mind. Both elements make a clear distinction between Russian and Italian futurism possible.

Italian futurism had a sociological slant, and tried to develop a literature that agreed with the technical world of today. New literary and aesthetic forms became necessary, because otherwise neither literature nor art were capable of creating an adequate world of expression, and such a situation would hamper the historical development of a culture. Frequent use of words such as 'electricity', 'propellor', 'radio', indicates a certain naiveté where more fundamental philosophical and sociological questions are concerned. Jakobson is thus being critical of Italian futurism by saying that it produces no more than a new technique of reporting, not a fundamental renewal of (poetical) language. Italian futurism tries to adapt vocabulary, Russian futurism on the other hand seeks the renewal of linguistics. Social dynamics plays a major rôle here, a problem that reappears in many forms, in Russian formalism, in the discussions with Marxism, and in the further developments of Czech structuralism, Social dynamics are not viewed here as being a one-sidedly sociological problem but in a holistic context in which the newly developing linguistics is eminently important. This perspective could, in itself, be taken as a forerunner of the modern structuralist approach. After all, Lévi-Strauss himself obviously considers linguistic elements and structures as characteristic components of a comprehensive epistemology of what is social. "Phonology has to play the same rôle as innovator for the social sciences as for instance nuclear physics plays for the whole field of the exact sciences", he says in his *Structural Anthropology*. Boris Eichenbaum, as early as 1925, when reviewing the connexion between futurism and formalism, wrote:

"We were determined to oppose the subjectivist aesthetic axioms of the symbolists by an objective scientific approach to the facts. The new pathos of scientific positivism that characterized the formalists springs from this; the philosophical and aesthetic presumptions were renounced". (*2.2*, 73)

It was, however, not only the formalist artists who were imbued with these principles. We come upon important common ground here between Russian formalism and other aesthetic movements of that time, the most important being cubism. It is remarkable how the spiritual climate of Europe then presented a unity, embracing not only art and literature but also science and philosophy.

The relationship between formalism and cubism in particular could be regarded as the hub of the approaches to the art, the philosophy, and the science of the time. Cubism was indeed not only to be found in painting, but also in literature (especially in English: James Joyce and Gertrude Stein should be mentioned here) and in music (Igor Stravinsky is an example). There was not only a French cubism but for a time also a Russian cubism, especially in painting, although certain futuristic beginnings in Russian poetry might also be mentioned in this regard. In addition, the theoretical propositions of cubism rested upon ethnological material as much as did formalistic linguistic research. As examples may be mentioned the analyses and studies of Negro art undertaken by Picasso and Juan Gris. The theoretical problems of the cubists were exactly the same as those formulated by Eichenbaum: demolition of the natural order of the material, and conscious reconstruction. The autonomous value of the basic elements of the material lying within the field of observation is also emphasized. In 1959, the well-known art-dealer and promotor of the early cubist painters, Daniel Henry Kahnweiler, author of the hitherto most significant biography of Juan Gris, wrote an essay, *Negerkunst und Kubismus,* in which he stressed that the cubists recognised in Negro art their own conception of a work of art as an autonomous object — Negro art necessarily uses signs, in all component details as well as in the totality. Consequently, the cubists focus upon the authenticity and the autonomy of what is pictured, not on a portrayal. They do not concentrate on a 'copy' but rather on a complex of meanings, in which the relation with the outside world is consciously constructed and manipulated. The only existing parallel to this is language. This philosophically clear concept explains the cubist painters' affinity for using script in their canvases, which certainly has nothing to do with decorative mannerisms, but with expressing their interpretation of the linguistic character of their art.

In this connexion, we should recall that cubism went through two stages: the analytic and the synthetic stage. The analytic stage includes the attempt to reject any resemblance to Nature, or what has become natural, in favour of the constructive process in artistic consciousness. By means of analysis, an attempt is made to emphasize how a work of art obeys its own laws. Inherent in any work of art is its own authentic order. If one wishes to use the word 'essence', as derived from idealist aesthetics, one would have to say that the essence of a work of art, as shown by that work itself, is its 'order'. Reproduction of the physical world thus has no value. Instead, the elements of such 'language' as is able to express this order are revealed — for the cubists they are the well-known cubes, planes, or facets. The later synthetic cubism tries to retain this 'language' but to make the structure more complex. Lévi-Strauss, in an interview in *The Sunday Times* (15.11.1970) during a visit to England, made a similar distinction between the analytic structuralism of Jakobson and Trubetzkoy and the synthetic structuralism of Chomsky. This observation is interesting to us here, because the phonology of Jakobson and Trubetzkoy did indeed identify phonemes as elements of language, and built structures with them. And a more synthetic interpretation did indeed only become possible with Chomsky. For structuralist activity, just like cubist activity, may be defined by using two typical operations: by 'separating out into elements', and by 'arrangement'. Barthes applies downright cubist concepts:

As soon as one takes the object apart, one discovers loose fragments of it, with minute differences between them from which a certain significance emerges. The fragment has no meaning in itself, but is so constituted that the smallest change one thinks of in its position or form produces a change in the whole. A *quadrangle* of Mondriaan, a *series* of Pousseur, a *line* in Butor's *Mobile,* a *mythem* of Lévi-Strauss, the *phoneme* of phonologists, the *theme* of some or other literary critic — all these units have a significant existence because of their very boundaries — as much because of boundaries that separate them from other existing units (a problem of the arrangement) as well as because of the boundaries that distinguish them from other *possible* units belonging to a similarly defined class... Structural man has either to define the rules of association from the units or to allocate such rules to them. This is the activity of arranging which follows upon the activity of designation... The regular recurrence of units, and associations of units, produces the work as a construct invested with significance.Linguists call the rules of such combinations *forms*; and it is advisable to keep to this strict use of such a hackneyed term. Form, it is said, is that which permits the contiguousness of units to appear as more than merely coincidental. A work of art is what rescues man from coincidence. (*4.10,* 193)

Eichenbaum, in his above-mentioned statement, also spoke of an objective scientific attitude towards facts. This claim was clearly made particularly in the early phenomenology, at the time of Husserl's *Logische Untersuchungen.* Phenomenology shares a positivist approach to facts with the manifesto's and protests of the Russian futurists, and with the theoretical statements of futurists and cubists. An anti-psychologistic frame of mind was their hall-mark. But one should guard against misunderstanding: Husserl was interested in a new, phenomenologically-oriented psychology, founded on the idea of the intentionality of consciousness, thus enabling it to take a stand against dogmatic behaviourism and stimulus-response psychology. Accordingly, linguistic researchers were not in the first place interested in the negation of certain kinds of psychology, but in a positivistic attitude towards facts and, closely related to this, in the theory of intentional consciousness.

This intentionality is a phenomenological formula for the constitutive capacity of the human mind which had already captured the main interest of futurists and formalists. For Husserl too the purposeful productive capacity of mind becomes apparent when man is the subject of language, i.e. with man as a being who creates language. At the same time a danger of a new psychologising arises, because the doctrine of the constitutive consciousness and its intentional products may be taken up in a neo-Kantian just as well as in a dogmatic-idealistic sense. One thus encounters, both in the *Logische Untersuchungen* and in the later *Formale und transzendentale Logik,* 1929, a non-resolved tension between a theory of constitutive consciousness on the one hand, and a philosophy of constituted semiological systems on the other.

The Moscow Circle ardently discussed precisely this phenomenological problem: the destinies of the early linguists were more closely related to philosophy than one generally concedes. Gustav Špet in particular spoke up for phenomenology in Russia, and tried to render the results of the *Logische Untersuchungen* profitable for linguistics. It was not so much anti-psychologism that was at issue, but mainly Husserl's notion of a 'pure grammar'. The very idea of this represents a conscious return to the rationalism of the seventeenth and eighteenth centuries. Language may thus possibly be seen, not only in a poetic or cubist light, but also philosophically as a system of signs. Other linguists such as Masaryk and Marty, emanating like Husserl from the school of Brentano, passed these ideas on, so that even in those years the thoughts of the Prague School, especially because of Mathesius, began to take form. Because of its universalism, the idea of a pure grammar linked up with the comparative and ethnographical tradition of the Moscow linguistics. Because of its positivist approach to ethnolinguistic facts, linguistics drew new inspiration from this. It once more became clear that language needed a synchronic description — in the same sense as Husserl had explained for psychology — and that linguistic elements should accordingly be considered as entities and not as bearers of psychic properties.

Husserl also developed a theory concerning the relationship between object and meaning. This linked up with futurist and symbolist conceptions of the capacity, in a linguistic work of art, of being interpreted in several ways. Meaning is always a linguistic phenomenon. Whatever abstract, object-less, distorted language might be presented as poetical or literary language, it always represents a field of meaning. We already see here what the Prague School will in due course emphasize more clearly : between the universe of objects and that of the emotional experiences of the reader there is a neutral and independent territory, viz. the territory of language. Linguistics and literary science are concerned with this territory only. If it is to be properly accessible, however, one is obliged to enter the field of tension between constitutive consciousness and constituted systems of signs.

2. RUSSIAN FORMALISM

All of this fell to the task of Russian formalism. Furthermore, futurism gave rise to the need for a scientific poetry — the formalist movement especially concerned itself with the principles of such poetry. General methodological problems were far more important to it than conclusions regarding scientific poetry, since they have outlived formalism and are still being debated in structuralism today.

The history of formalism, recorded by Erlich in his monograph (*2.3*), is closely connected with theories and destinies of the Petersburg and Moscow Circles, as well as with the gradual ascendency of totalitarian Marxism. The years 1916 to 1920 are the period in which formalist theory was developed — the theories of the Petersburg Circle, known as *Opojaz*, are especially important. There was, however, close cooperation with the Moscow Circle — only afterwards did the interests of the two circles slightly diverge. The Moscovites were more interested in linguistic problems, the Petersburgers in questions concerning the theory of literature. In those times, the main theoretical problems were poetical procedure *(priëm)*, alienation *(ostranenije)*, and literary form. The ensuing period, 1921-1926, is the period in which the insights that had been gained were thoroughly explored and tested. The discussion with Marxism, and the deeper-going study of form, became especially important. After all, formalist theory originated in a continuous dialogue, not only with its many opponents, but also between one formalist and another (themselves opposing and criticising each other). Significantly different viewpoints are thus encountered. Striedter says in this regard:

The linguists Jakobson and Jakubinsky, the literary historians Eichenbaum and Tynjanow, the theoretician and political writer Sklovsky, the specialist in verse Tomasevsky, and Brik (important as organizer and debater) — to name only the most important of the first decade – were all at the same time partners and opponents in the fascinating dialogue that created and developed the formal method. The big chance lay here – to overcome, in the course of the work itself, the initial shortcomings inherent in an empiricism that had not been adequately tested methodologically. Formalism used this chance intensively, although it was obviously not able, during its short history and in view of internal and external difficulties, to discuss all relevant questions fully or even to formulate them clearly. (*2.20*, XVIff.)

The years 1926 to 1930 may be regarded as the period of crisis and collapse. On the one hand, the orthodox Opojaz-teachings did not manage to revise the over-subtle formalistic principles, whereas on the other hand their philosophical immaturity, when confronted by Marxists and other opponents, turned out to be fatal. In 1928, Jakobson and Tynjanov once again summarised the available results, and by so doing designed a 'Summa' of formalist thinking. They tried in their theses to evade extreme empiricism and dogmatic formalism by an attempt at establishing a closer relationship between aesthetic principles and other vectors of culture. This could have resulted in the development of a new Russian formalism or even in structuralism, but the historical situation operated decisively against such revification. These theses, therefore, could not be developed fully until they emigrated from Russia and were espoused particularly by the Prague School. At that time Russian literature was already being made to toe the line, just like critique and the theory of literature. The time for experiments in a non-Marxist sense had gone. The first Five Year Plan started on its course, and the so-called RAPP (Russian Association of Proletarian Writers) gradually dominated the whole literary scene.

We now turn first to the most important elements of the Opojaz theories – procedure, alienation, form – returning later to the relationship between Formalism and Marxism. Both Opojaz and Marxism are indeed directly relevant, not only for the Czech version of structuralism, but also for structuralism today.

A. *Procedure*

Henceforth, taking Jakobson's and Striedter's advice, we translate 'priëm' by 'procedure' and not by 'device' or 'artifice', as was done in the German translation by Erlich and afterwards in the translated works of Eichenbaum, Tynjanov, Sklovsky, and Mukařovsky. Among the catchwords of the Opojaz theories were *priëm ostranenija* (procedure of alienation), *obnaženie priëm* (revealed procedure), or the general statement: "the literary work is the sum of the total artistic procedures applied therein". These expressions are not without philosophical and aesthetic relevance. Had the usual term 'means of expression' been employed, a psychologism would once again have appeared, because the use of that term suggests that poetry reveals the mind of the poet. A theory pre-supposing there might be such a 'mind' and such a 'poet' could anyhow never have developed into a formalistic theory.

According to the Opojaz, all art is the result of a technical intervention, never the result of a mere presentation. This has consequences pertaining to language as well as pertaining to reality. The technique of a consciously-made work of art relates directly to the *formation* of material – the language in the case of the poet – and to the deformation of the matter – reality. Everything else – emotional content, ideologies, psychological make-up of the characters – is usually considered to be 'post factum motivation' of the applied priëm. The later, orthodox, Opojaz theory even sought to dispute the relevance of sociological and ideological considerations where a work of art was concerned, thus rendering the theory particularly vulnerable to Marxism. This point of departure has three important implications.

Firstly, it becomes clear that the problems of artistic procedure do not stand on their own, but are elements of a more complex totality, problems of alienation, form, and function being closely related to *priëm*. If, as the Opojaz theorists maintain, the literary work of art is the sum total of the procedures applied therein, then the question arises whether the analysis of artistic procedure, which extracts one factor out of this whole complex, should be an analysis of structure or an analysis of function. Tynjanov says in this regard:

The entity of a work is not a closed, symmetrical entity, but a gradually developing, dynamic one. Between its component parts, the law of correlation and integration is applicable, not the law of equality or addition.

Elsewhere he says:

It pays to analyse single elements of a work, such as subject, style, rhythm, and syntaxis in prose, or rhythm and semantics in poetry. Such analysis leads us to realise that such elements can be rendered abstract within the limited framework of a working hypothesis. At the same time, however, we are led to understand that all these elements are inherently synchronised, and that they react upon one another. Anybody who explores rhythm in verse and then rhythm in prose inevitably discovers that the rôles of the same element in different systems are different. (*2.2.* 41; *2.25,* 41)

Tynjanov, therefore, clearly has an analysis of function in mind if light is to be shed upon the structure of a work of art. His distinctions are based upon the fundamental view (originating in formalism and greatly influencing later Czech as well as modern structuralism) that "a work of literature is a system, just like the whole of literature is a system". One could say, as Tynjanov does: A system of systems.

Secondly, this approach to artistic procedure implies renunciation of

normative aesthetics. It is very important to bear this renunciation in mind,
so that the relativism in formalistic structuralist thinking is not overlooked.
Why this thinking is irreconcilable with normative aesthetics, and with *a
priori* norms in general, is a far-reaching philosophical question. We should
not, however, forget that a fundamental presupposition in any formalistic/
structuralistic analysis is the equivalence of the elements analysed. Such
equivalence is never to be found in normative aesthetics. For the same reason,
a similar renunciation can be noted in related artistic systems like futurism
and cubism, or, simultaneously, in Russian poetry of that era.

Thirdly, the analysis of artistic procedure *(priëm)* stresses occurrences as
conscious occurrences, and hence as technical interventions. Techniques and
consciousness are posited as essential elements of creativity, and are thus
presuppositions in any formalist or structuralist approach. According to
Barthes (in his essay on structuralist activity that has often been cited, viz.
L'activité structuraliste) Opojaz-theories equally presuppose them. Barthes
notes that technique is the essence of all creation. Structuralism is thus dis-
tinct from other types of analysis or creation because the object is put together in a new fashion so as to make functions apparent. This formula
sounds like a synopsis of those Opojaz theories that apply to procedure. The
ideas of priëm are *formation* and *deformation*; those of the structuralist
'activité' are *arrangement* and *analysis*.

Consequently, concrete procedure (as *priëm*) resembles structuralist activity (as *activité*). Sklovsky, in his programmatic 1916 essay *Art as Procedure
(2.10)*, stresses that one should do without the usual observations of empirical conformities as well as without the procedure of stating and verifying
hypotheses about laws. The procedure which is implicit in the material itself
permits conclusions to be drawn about the structures and effects of literature, with which the historical material might eventually then be compared.
Sklovsky tries to apply these principles in particular to a literary genre which
until then had been regarded as belonging to studies in folklore rather than
studies in literature, viz. the fairy tale. Because it is seldom clear precisely
what the actual subject is of a fairy tale, the fairy tale itself cannot, if criteria
of an idealistically aesthetic nature are employed, be regarded as the expression of a specific creative personality. For this reason, the Opojaz-theorists
regarded the fairy tale as a test of their views — the use of language appears
here as a specific system. Specific structures function in this system; and
they in turn are coordinated in a system of systems, i.e. the relevant literature. In this way, laws regarding structure, by means of which we are able to
understand the relevant literature, become apparent. Vladimir Propp (*Mor-
phology of the Fairy Tale*, 1928) is usually the model for such analyses of

priëm. According to him, neither the subjects nor the motives of a fairy tale can explain its specific unity. They are, on the contrary, interchangeable elements in the structure of the whole, whose position and function from time to time are determined by a constant structural principle. As early as in 1926, Nikiforov had suggested regarding individual 'narrative actions', as well as their interrelations within the composition, as if they were words in a language. This linguistic key makes the discovery of constant structures in composition possible. Propp's and Nikiforov's analyses closely resemble the principles of Greimas's *Semantique structurale*, 1966. Works in the field of general semiotics (particularly relating to mythologies), studies on the literary subject, structuralist research into literary genres — all draw inspiration from this source. The technique of this procedure is mirrored in Roland Barthes's analysis of *Sarrasine,* a text by Honoré de Balzac. Barthes's analysis, published in 1970, bears the somewhat enigmatic title: *S/Z*. A key to this title may be found in the well-known essay on structuralist activity (*L'activité structuraliste*, 1963) in which we read that:

Two units of a paradigm must in some respect be similar, so that the dissimilarity which distinguishes them may become apparent. S and Z have at the same time to possess a common property (their dentality) and a distinctive property (presence or absence of sonority) ... The analysis therefore first brings about a shattering of the object, but the units of the structure are thereby certainly not themselves shattered — before they are divided up and subsumed into the composition, every one of them creates, together with what could possibly belong to it, an intelligent organism, subject to a sovereign dynamic principle; the principle of the smallest difference. (*4.11*, 217)

Many analyses of modern French literary structuralism, particularly those from the Circle around the review *Tel Quel*, deal with this question and are characterized by this procedure.

It should be noted that questions as to what the 'essence' is of the creative personality are set aside in favour of the 'handling' of the language, i.e. its literary technology. Literature is taken as a semiotic phenomenon, and there is thus no room for a psychology of the mind of the creative subject. We are concerned, rather, with literary-technical functions and conventions. As with de Saussure, the conventional element is emphasized, and poetry viewed as an already ordered system of signs. This raises the question of the aesthetic *modus operandi*; of how indeed the literary work is arrived at. Analysis and taking apart, as well as alienation and procedure, are subject to this structuralist principle. This may already be seen in the titles of the formalist Opojaz-analyses — Eichenbaum's essay for instance on *How Gogol's Cloak was Made,* or Sklovsky's analysis of *How Don Quixote was Made (2.10).* Not only in these works but also in today's structuralist thinking the demand for a *modus operandi* remains highly relevant.

B. *Alienation*

The concept of alienation is deeply rooted in the literary tradition of Russian intellectual life. Dissimilar movements such as romanticism, symbolism, futurism, formalism and Marxism are linked by this concept. Alienation as a specific aesthetic procedure, *priëm ostranenija,* is the formalist theme which comes fully fledged from Sklovsky's early essay on *Art as Procedure.* In romanticism and symbolism it is merely a matter of a literary technique, in which the subject takes the world apart. Symbolism interprets this as coming about through a rampant subjective fantasy, but for futurism it comes about through conscious provocation. Formalism, however, looks for much more – it regards the constitutive rôle of the subject in the process of alienation as itself a part of a wider process. This involves taking a fundamentally anti-idealistic step: the subject's obvious autonomy together with its constitutive capacity cease to be the only theoretical points of departure.

Sklovsky's theory of alienation chiefly sets out to put an end to treating observation as if it were automatic. In his discussions of the theory of literature, Sklovsky thus shifts the accent to the function of the image and to its wider connotations. The poetic image then appears as no more than one of the procedures at the disposal of the poet, and no meaning is ascribable to the image in itself. It is the function of the image (i.e. its structural context) that makes the meaning clear. This gives rise to a shift in semantic emphasis, opening the way to a comprehensive structural theory of alienation. In the above-mentioned essay, Sklovsky says:

Things one repeatedly sees one begins by means of recognition truly to observe: the object is before us, we know about it, but we fail to see it. We can't, therefore, say anything about it. In art, the object can, by several means, be rescued from automatic observation.

Elsewhere he adds:

That which one calls art exists to feel things, to render the stone stonier. It is art's objective to help us really to *see* an object, not merely to *recognize* it. The artistic procedure is the 'alienation' of things, bringing about a more complicated form. This procedure increases the intricacy and the duration of the observation, because the process of observation in art is in itself an objective and must be intensified. Art is a means to experience the making of a thing; what, however, is made is not important in art. (*2.3,* 15)

Particularly by using a structural analysis of Tolstoy's prose, Sklovsky tries to demonstrate that the automation of our whole process of observation is brought about by the rôle of the constitutive subject. In Tolstoy's work, a procedure to avoid this automation is to be found which Sklovsky mentions as an example for *priëm ostranenija,* An object is not signified by its name. This is of great linguistic relevance: do objects have a name, are names expressions that have to do with the essence of the object, or are they just conventional signs for them? Instead of referring to an object by its name, Tolstoy describes it as if it were being observed for the first time, or as if an incident were occurring for the first time. This is a change in orientation, in which the psychological shock effect ought to lead us back to the original experience. This is probably a somewhat naïve psychology. Tolstoy, in his description of an object, does not indicate its constituent parts by employing concepts derived directly from the totality of the subject, but calls them instead by the names by which corresponding parts of other things might be known — thus the alienation, brought about by a structural description based upon the view that meanings can only stem from the place and function of elements in a totality. Tolstoy also introduces an outsider into his stories, so that things become alienated by employing the ways of observation of an outsider, not our own ways. Striedter remarks that Tolstoy never used this difficult procedure in his plays; not, in other words, when it was a matter of the real action of a subject. There could be two reasons for this: it was clear to Tolstoy, and also to Sklovsky, that the alienation process involved difficult literary-aesthetic complications. Also, for Tolstoy and the later formalists the process of alienation was an aesthetic issue, not an ethical one. This second reason led Brecht, after his visit to Russia in 1936, to attribute more value to the ethical relevance of alienation (which he learned from Sklovsky at the time) than to its aesthetic relevance. This led him to present alienation on the stage. For the rest, the formalist conception of alienation differs from Tolstoy's process. The alienation of the whole narrative context is necessary, because only in this way can our recognition be freed from automatism and can the original precision (Russian: *faktura*) of our observation be regained.

For formalists too, therefore, alienation goes beyond what is merely aesthetic, not so much in ethical respects, however, as in epistemological ones. Linguistics is the model for this change. For this reason, Jakobson, in a 1933 essay entitled 'On Poetry', stressed that it was the task of literature in general and poetry in particular (in contradistinction to 'poetical language') to remind us that a sign is never identical with the object it refers to, but that on the other hand a certain measure of correspondence between the two must exist. When thinking about the identity of the sign and that of the signified object, the imperfections of both identities have to be borne in mind. The reader has constantly to be reminded of such imperfections. This implies an argument against a romantic, idealistic interpretation, because

Jakobson does not see alienation solely in the constitutive consciousness of the reader and his attitude towards reality, but recognises it as a linguistic fact. This must be made clear to the reader, so that he does not think of himself as the cause of the alienation. What seems to be founded upon the attitude of the reader is indeed an independent linguistic fact. To make this fact clear, a literary device is necessary — what the formalists call 'formation' and 'deformation', or, as Barthes has it, 'arrangement' and 'taking apart'.

C. Form

We might take it as a matter of course that, in Opojaz theories as well as in latter-day formalism, in Czech as well as in present-day structuralism, the problem of literary form plays an important rôle. The point of departure is the insight, derived from linguistics, into the autonomous value-structure of the word. At the same time, the communicative function of a language is, to much greater extent, regarded as being relative, especially in poetical language but also in practical language. Jakobson, in his essay 'On Poetry' (1933) says: "The special characteristic of poetry is that a word is observed as a word, not only as representing an indicated object or an expression of emotion — that words and their sequence, their meaning, their external and internal form, acquire their proper weight and value."

The autonomy of the word raises the question of the specificity of literary material: What is actually the poet's material? This question illustrates the new formalist orientation. Formerly, a question like this would have been considered pointless, or would have been shrugged off with the traditional reference to the problem of form and content. The question, however, isn't directed at the distinction between the content of literature and its form, but at 'how literature is made', i.e. at principles of ordering and construction. The very form of the question is characteristic of formalism. No longer is form seen *a priori* as a receptacle into which the content is poured. The material is indeed to be recognised in its autonomy, in that the properties of the material stem from its *use*. The old scheme of form and content therefore becomes valueless. Content, *in itself,* is nothing; only usage counts (i.e. the functional network of relationships makes the material appear as content). In this way, the problems of form are fundamentally associated with the problems of procedure *(priëm)* and function.

This structuralist conception *avant la lettre* is particularly clearly illustrated by Sklovsky and Tynjanov. The former emphasizes the connexion between artistic forms and other, already extant, forms. Tynjanov, on the strength of these views, designs a dynamic theory of literary evolution which might lay claim to being a structuralist sociology of literature.

Sklovsky, in an earlier essay ('The Interconnexion between the Procedure of Building a Subject and General Procedure in Style', 1916) states that even the form of a work of art has itself a structural relation to other forms that already exist. Thus a general rule is also applicable here: "... Every work of art is created as a parallel and a contrast to an available model. A new form is not created to express a new content, but to take over from an old form that has lost its character as an artistic form." This does not mean that the sequence or even the genetic order is automatic, but only that structural relationships set literary form in a true light, i.e. as one fact in a more comprehensive context of equivalent facts. Every work of art is a form, every form has a *differentiating quality*, a concept employed by the German aesthetic Broder Christiansen (*Philosophie der Kunst*, 1909), which can only function within the context of the relevant forms.

Boris Eichenbaum carries this further in his 1925 study, 'The Theory of Formal Method'. First, he approvingly quotes Tynjanov's remarks in 'The Problem of Poetic Language' (1924), stressing that the material used in verbal art is heterogeneous and of uneven value.

Often one single moment may take precedence over all others. [But] the concept of the 'material' remains within the realm of form; it is formal itself. It is a mistake to confuse it with non-constructive moments ... the unity of a work is not a closed symmetrical unity, but a slowly unfolding and thus dynamic unity. The law of correlation and integration, not that of equity or addition, applies to its parts. The form of a work of literature is dynamic.

Eichenbaum adds that the evolution of literature should itself be seen as a specific set in the network of other sets within a culture. While this on the one hand subjects the dynamics of literary evolution to historical laws, it also characterizes literature as a specific social phenomenon. Tynjanov once again emphasizes the structuralist view when he says:

The characteristic quality of a literary work exists in the application of a constructive factor to material – thus in the formation (or more precisely in the deformation or taking apart) of this material. The constructive factor does not merge into the material, neither does it 'comply with' it. It is, however, connected to the material in an 'eccentric' way – it emerges from the material. It is clear that 'material' and 'form' are not opposed to one another. The material itself is 'formal', because *there is no material without the construction.* (2.2, 19; author's italics)

Two problems are presaged in these statements: (i) the later developments particularly of Czech structuralism (discussed in detail especially by Jan Mukařovský) i.e. the problem of the literary subject or the literary individuality; and (ii) structuralist treatment of the relationships between literature and society, a functional analysis of considerable complexity. The works of Šklovsky, Tynjanov, and Eichenbaum offer the most valuable material in this regard.

Summarizing, one could say that in Russian formalism a structuralist approach is already to be seen, determined particularly by phonological and linguistic findings. Opojaz-theoreticians considered literature as a semiological system, and they undertook a functional and systems analysis, albeit piecemeal. In this way, a literary technology came into being, characteristic of present-day structuralism.

3. FORMALISM AND MARXISM

It is a rather remarkable historical fact that, in the very period in which Marxist thinking became the dominant doctrine, the Opojaz theoreticians developed a theory of literature which neglected the connexion between literature and society. At the height of the Opojaz developments, between 1920 and 1925, we find a debate with Marxism, which was not abandoned until near the end of the decade, when Marxism had become a comprehensive dogma. Among the Prague structuralists, this discussion was maintained over a longer period. After the Second World War and after the extentialist period, the discussion with the Marxists was again resumed, this time mainly in French structuralism. Whereas, in the early stages of the debate, Marxism and formalism were clearly opposed to one another, latterly the discussion concerns itself more with a structuralist conception of Marxism.

We turn first to the Marxists' discussions with the Opojaz theorists. What set these discussions off was the indifference of the Opojaz approach to the connexions between literature and society. Sklovsky's presumptuous statement, dating from 1923, is often quoted as an example of this: "Art has always been independent of life and its colour has never reflected the colour of the flag that fluttered over the city bastions."

No formalist would probably have taken such an exaggerated formulation seriously, all the more because, some years later, Tynjanov, Eichenbaum, and others treated the relation between literature and society as a structural philosophy — indeed, as a system of systems.

The manifest reason for this change in the middle of the decade was certainly the on-going debate with Marxism, but the latent reason must nevertheless have been preponderant — the necessity, that is, (starting with the problem of form, and taking into account the difficulties created by the way a strict linguistic scheme would classify literary material) of increasing the complexity of the structural approach and of examining the connexions between literary and non-literary elements. This implied new themes, such as for instance the motivation of a work of art, the structure of societal factors influencing literary evolution, the problems of the creative personality, the characteristics of the literary genre that is without specific subject (fairy tales, riddles, and myths — according to Propp) as well as the difference between the so-called folk tale and the 'artistic' fairy tale such as Andersen for instance writes. Thus elements were introduced into formalist thinking which offered a basis for discussion with the Marxists.

We should note that formalism, off its own bat, turned against all tendencies to see literature as a medium for any extra-literary factor. The autonomy of literature as the art of words does not represent a polemic attitude towards Marxism, but rather an independent achievement of formalist thinking itself. From this point of view too, a genuine discussion with Marxism would have been fruitful. But in the second half of the decade it was already too late for that — history had already made an open discussion impossible. Marxist opponents clung to their dogmatic convictions re basis and superstructure, and it was only after the liberalization Stalin achieved in 1950 — his Pravda articles on Marxism and linguistic problems played a major part in this — that it became possible to conclude differently.

The most important document in the first stage of the argument between the Marxists and the Opojaz theorists is Leo Trotzky's book *Literature and Revolution* (1924). It turned out to be the most translated and thus the best-known work, and Erlich's study, which cited other (unpublished) material, reinforces the impression that Trotsky's book has the most to offer. Outside Russia, the Italian aesthete and philosopher Galvano Della Volpe (1895-1968) offered a more searching critique of Trotsky's critique of formalism (*Critica dell' ideologia contemporanea*, 1967). More than a third of Trotsky's book is a polemic treatise on futurism and formalism. And, although he is extremely critical, he does grant a certain measure of recognition to the merits of formalism. These Trotzky sees particularly in connexion with technical questions in the theory of literature. He states clearly that formalism as a philosophy, as aesthetics, or even as an outlook on life is absolutely incompatible with Marxism, and makes this the point of his attacks. Trotzky, moreover, had not yet been bound by the concept, later to become intransigent dogma, of literature as a mirror of life or as a way of registering social phenomena. This mirror theory, dominating Marxist aesthetics for so long, is softened in Trotzky's case by the insight that a certain distortion of reality may well belong to the special rules of art. The autonomy of the work of art as opposed to reality is at the same time thus in the main accepted. Trotzky has to admit this autonomy, because Marxism is not in a position to pass aesthetic judgment on certain schools of art in a certain historical period. It can only explain them. The question why a certain form of art appears at a certain time indeed is not answered by formalism either —

the question is not even put. Trotzky's explanation for this is very interesting. He tries to argue that formalism itself is neither philosophy, nor ideology, nor *Weltanschauung*; it is nothing but a revision of Neo-Kantianism. Trotzky thus steers formalist thinking back to the field, familiar to him, of philosophical idealism, and reveals formalism as being a Neo-Kantian fallacy.

This criticism was meant to be devastating, and it indeed had great influence on the more dogmatic critics of formalism. Its attraction was apparently so strong that even Erlich, in his monograph on Russian Formalism, adds to his statement of Trotzky's point of view: "... not without a certain justification ..." (*2.13*, 114). He does not, however, tell us why he thinks Trotzky may have been justified.

In our view, the opinion that the philosophy of formalism is Neo-Kantian is entirely erroneous. It is interesting to note that the same allegation is to be found in philosophical interpretations of cubism of the French type, especially in Daniel Henry Kahnweiler's biography of Juan Gris, in which he presents cubism as *peinture conceptuelle*. It is also to be found in Gehlen's interpretations of cubist painting. As early as 1962, Gadamer said in this regard: "How absurd is the idea that cubism brought about the synthesis of of apperception in the picture, and that the anything but revolutionary Neo-Kantianism created, shortly before its blessed death, the greatest revolution of European painting since Giotto. Nothing could be more incredible." The remark applies here too. We can understand that an allegation of being Neo-Kantian was made against formalism and cubism, since both (as has already been explained) have the same philosophical presuppositions, play similar rôles in the rejuvenation of European art, and show close relation to each other. The fallacy emanates from the fact, simple in itself, that the decentralization of the rôle of the subject in formalism and cubism has not been recognized, nor has anybody wanted to recognize it. What was taken for granted in any idealist philosophy, viz. that the subject is the point of departure, is dispensed with by the formalists and the cubists, Only thus did a relativist philosophy, as well as aesthetics as practised by formalism and cubism, become possible. Both are based on the notion that the order of every relevant element *has not been established:* the philosophical subject also belongs to such elements. There are many ways in which the order may be devined, and each results in a different perspective. Trotzky did not see the philosophical implications of *renouncing an established order* as the basis for philosophy and aesthetics, nor did he see the implications of *treating 'order' itself as the main problem.* But herein lies the philosophical consequence of any structural philosophy — it concerns the equivalence of elements and perspectives that inevitably results from abandoning a fixed point of view in favour of a variable one. For this reason, the very similar problems of linguistics are philosophically relevant. 'Language' and 'game' are important metaphors of modern philosophy. They are one another's reflected image. The theme of 'order' seems always central here. The formalist search for 'elements', 'phonemes', 'poetic material', the conviction that meanings have a conventional character — all these are based on one and the same philosophical insight, namely that the problem of order can itself become a theme. Formalist thinkers had already emphasized (as Wittgenstein later was to do) the *use* of words in the language from which their *function* results. This use is *vérité de fait* of all human experience of the world. The *ordo* can only be discovered in the use of, for instance, language, a game, or the elements of art. Hence the justified formalist question: 'How is it made?' Hence also the structuralist requirement 'to bring out the functions'. The formalist-structuralist approach confirms the philosophical view that people do not speak, think, or create art only *according to* schemes of order, but that people speak, think, or create art *by means of* schemes of order. Only in this way can the revolutionary rôle of formalism and cubism, or the nature of today's structuralism, be understood. This light on the philosophical consequences of the formalist point of view was not only necessary to contradict Trotzky's thesis but also to stress the philosophical importance of the formalist and structuralist effort. We are today still far from regarding structuralism as a current in philosophy. Nonetheless, formalism must be seen as a timid first attempt at breaking through to a language *about* order, and to a game *with* order, without formalism itself possessing definitive criteria *for* order. This is demonstrated by the interest in a literary genre of which the subject cannot be identified as fixed — in such a genre, the autonomy of the subject is supplanted by an anonymous structure. The principal eccentricity of structural thinking and systems thinking is here explified.

Because of this eccentricity, Marxism indeed had to oppose formalist thinking. Marxism has a perspective and knows about an order that ought to be there. Trotzky therefore repeatedly polemicizes against the formalist idea of alienation, which he labels as escapism. The concept of distortion, akin to the concept of alienation, leads, according to him, to a complete denial of the social and historical meaning of the process of alienation, and to another kind of distortion, i.e. distortion of the artist's awareness of his social responsibility. The task of art in society would be unrecognizably caricatured if social, historical, and linguistic material were at the free disposal of the artist to create a new world out of them. Trotzky does not understand the functional aspect of this procedure. His interpretation of the formalist's view is authoritarian, as if the artist really could dispose freely and idiosyncratically over all of that, and as if the world were, by virtue of his art, delivered into his power. Instead of this, functionalistic formalism accentuates the free disposability not only of the object but also of the subject. Consequently, the subject is not something autonomously constituted — rather, in a profound sense, it is *in the game*. Thus, in the same year as Trotzky's book appeared, Eichenbaum could reply that Marxism and formalism were different conceptions. Marxism was a philosophy, especially a philosophy of history — formalism did not have such a framework at its disposal and it was thus no more than one school of thought within the theory of literature.

Modern Russian structuralism, which, once Stalin had gone, had a chance to develop, seeks to do away with the distinction between a holistic view and research into the details of the theory of literature. One of the most important representatives of this structuralism, Jurij M. Lotman, in his work *Struktura chudo zestvennogo teksta* (The Structure of the Artistic Text), published in Moscow in 1970, states that the analysis of the inner structure of the text always should be accompanied by an analysis of how the text functions within its total socio-cultural setting. One thus is led to a view of culture conceived of as a complex and controversial totality of hierarchically organized systems of signs. For Lotman, this in turn implies a fresh look at Russian formalism, and also at the contributions of the Prague linguistic school.

CHAPTER III

PRAGUE

In this chapter we examine to what extent Prague may be said to be the place of origin of present-day structuralist thought. In so far as the aesthetic isolationism of the Opojaz-theorists was abandoned, and literary work in particular examined in its societal context, formalism gave rise to structuralism, the principles contributed by formalism being retained. Art is fundamentally perceived as a semiological fact. Based upon this insight, connexions can be made with other semiological facts, thus adding to the complexity of the structural approach. Literature is thus no longer reduced to words only, nor identified exclusively with what is literary. It is in Czechoslovakian structuralism that for the first time the outline of the structural activity becomes clear.

1. CONSTELLATIONS

Since the beginning of the second decade, the outcomes of the discussions of the Moscow Circle and the broader Opojaz theorists have been generally known — outside Russia as well, and especially in Prague. The study of the basic principles of formalism was advanced there particularly by the linguist Vilém Mathesius. The phenomenology of language, as well as the study of its structure, occupied a frontal place in the general interest. Furthermore, the question of the inner structure of language (von Humboldt) became topical, and the distinction between poetical and practical language was discussed, as was the connexion between culture and these two types of language. These were all questions to which the active members of the Moscow Circle had contributed. When, in the summer of 1924, the Circle was dissolved — a few members having meanwhile transferred to the State Academy for the Study of the Arts — these themes had by no means been exhausted. The idea of looking at things structurally found its chief echo in Czechoslovakia. Since 1920, Roman Jakobson had been working in Prague. Thus, as early as March 1925 and ten years after the founding of the Moscow Circle, on the invitation of Mathesius, the possibility was being considered of a Prague Circle on the Moscow model. The official opening session of this Circle took place in the Karl University in Prague on 16 October 1926. The continuity of structural thinking was, at least as far as these external circum-

stances were concerned, guaranteed. Becker, a young German student of
language, gave an address on 'The European Spirit of Language' *(Der
europäische Sprachgeist)*. Subsequently, many similar sessions followed,
chiefly in the premises of the University but later — to emphasize independence — in the private venues of Prague's coffee houses. Many former members
of the Moscow Circle contributed.

Since 1929, the year of the first international Slavonic Congress in Prague
important works by his Circle have appeared under the French title
Travaux du Cercle Linguistique de Prague. Soon the name *Cercle Linguistique de Prague* was internationally known. From the outset, Jakobson favoured the French term *Cercle*, even in the language mixture of *Prager
Cercle*, so as not to create the impression of closure and exclusiveness which
the German word *Kreis* might have given rise to — as was, in his opinion, the
case with the *George-Kreis*.

In 1926, a Czech edition of Jakobson's 'On Czech Verse' *(Über den
tschechischen Vers)* appeared — that work which already three years earlier
had appeared simultaneously in Berlin (under the aegis of Maxim Gorki)
and in Moscow (in the Russian language, under the imprint of the Moscow
Circle). The point of view which it engendered influenced the debate which,
especially in Czechoslovakia, was being conducted about the extent to which
a qualitative or a quantitative metrical system was more appropriate in
Czech verse. Jakobson established that, seen from a linguistic point of view,
a quantitative metrical system was the most suitable. His analyses also
proved the relevance of phonemical elements in verse language, as it is indeed these which enable us to distinguish the meanings of words. In this
context, a distinction was for the first time established between significant
language elements in verse — a distinction to be intensified a decade later in
the phonemic studies of both Jakobson and Trubetzkoy. But it was not to
rest with a new linguistic and phonemic perspective: the aesthetic principle
of formalism also played an important rôle. Jakobson stressed that this
principle could provide a 'natural' basis for the very existence of poetry,
because the writing of poetry would always presuppose and manifest something artificial; aesthetic conventions would be consciously infused into the
word material. In this way the formalistic tradition had been given the floor
— to speak against speculative reflexions and explanations based on the
'spirit' of the relevant language, and in favour of the analytic and the con-
structivistic.

We may regard the thesis-like attempt of Jakobson and Tynjanov to put
together the formalistic content of the journal *Nowy Lef* (No. 12, 1928) as
being a second very important document for the Prague Circle. We draw

particular attention to these problems of research into literature and language for two reasons — in the first place because they sought a way out of the confines of a dogmatic formalism, and in the second place because they contain in concentrated form the results of Tynjanov's examination of the problems of literary and societal evolution (and thus the inquiry into the 'system of systems'). These viewpoints may indeed be regarded as the original mainspring of later Czech structuralism. Erlich even believes that these theses might have been able to form the theoretical foundation for a neoformalism — which is in contradistinction to the further works of an Eichenbaum or a Sklovsky.

In the same year (1928) the first International Congress on Linguistics took place in The Hague. Two groups, viz. representatives of Genevan linguistics (in the tradition of de Saussure) and representatives of the Prague Circle, found themselves meeting together to establish a general programme for a structural and functional linguistics. Phonology formed an essential ingredient of this Congress's remarkable contribution. This contribution, together with the above-mentioned theses of Tynjanov and Jakobson, to a certain extent formed the material of the Prague Circle's important *Theses* on the occasion of the first International Slavonic Congress in Prague in 1929. Jointly, they initiated the series of *Travaux du Cercle Linguistique de Prague,* making up a contribution with the non-commital title: *Mélanges linguistiques dédiés au premier congrès des philologues slaves.* Jakobson, Mukařovský, and Trubetzkoy were the chief authors of these documents, so important for the Prague Circle. Their content should be subjected to a closer analysis. In any case, the idea of a wider-ranging way of looking at a literary work of art was itself important. The close connexion between the theory of language and the theory of literature, as well as the relationship between the aesthetic and the other functions of language, provide evidence of this. The same thoughts are conveyed in the exposition of Prague linguistics, dated 1935, and published in the journal *Slovo a Slovesnost* — a journal which was closely connected with the Prague Circle.

In the same year, Husserl and Carnap were invited to address the Prague Circle. Carnap was very interested in the problem of language. The logico-positivist movement had expanded considerably since the Seventh International Philosophical Congress, held in Oxford in 1930. Because of the journal *Erkenntnis,* because of the concept of a unified science *(Einheitswissenschaft)* — which was to be translated into reality with the issue, in 1935, of the *International Encyclopaedia of Unified Science* — and also because of the close contacts between the Vienna and the Prague Circles, his invitation was more or less a matter of course. After all, it was he who, as early as

1928, in his book 'The Logical Construction of the World' *(Der logische Aufbau der Welt)*, had tackled the problem of structural description, had explored its possibility, had formulated examples, and had drawn the conclusion that fundamentally all scientific explanations were structural explanations.

Husserl's invitation, too, is not to be wondered at. It reminds us of the activities of the Moscow Circle and indicates the wide influence of his 'Logical Inquiries' *(Logische Untersuchungen)* enhanced by the book on 'Formal and Transcendental Logic' *(Formale und transzendentale Logik)* that appeared in 1929. At that time, Gustav Špet, the most important representative of phenomenology in Russia, established himself as phenomenologist primarily by an application and expansion of the concept of a 'pure' grammar. Špet, Marty, and Masaryk started off, like Husserl himself, in Brentano's school. Husserl spoke in Prague both at the Karl University and to the Prague Circle. His first address at the University took place on 14 November 1935; four days later he spoke to the *Cercle* on 'The Phenomenology of Language' *(Phänomenologie der Sprache)*. Both occasions were very successful. Husserl had in May of that year already given an address in Vienna on *Die Philosophie in der Krisis der europäischen Menschkeit*. In Prague, as in Vienna, he spoke *ex tempore*. On 12 December 1935, looking back on these addresses, he wrote to his boyhood friend Gustav Albrecht in Vienna: "What was done in Prague was greater, not only in that it represented a co-ordinated cycle, but also in that I, unprepared and thinking on my feet, had to address two scientific associations, on each occasion for two hours ..." The title mentioned here is based on the title of Husserl's speech to the Prague Circle. Among his hearers was Ludwig Landgrebe, at that time *Privatdozent* in the Karl University.

Frau Malvin Husserl, in a letter dated 23 October 1935, wrote to Roman Ingarden that the themes Husserl had to deal with in Prague were less precisely laid down "because he [Husserl] will deliver four lectures in Prague in the middle of November at the invitation of the *Cercle Philosophique* [this was *not* the Prague Circle!] ; Nature and Spirit — Natural Science, Cultural Science, Psychology, Phenomenology. How nice it would be if you too could come." That also in Prague there were various circles and various currents, is revealed in a further letter of Frau Husserl's. On 14 January 1936 she wrote to Roman Ingarden:

Prague was a complete success. Such a cordial, indeed enthusiastic reception from old and young, both German and Czech sides, could really not have been anticipated. My husband delivered a four-hour speech (the first half in the German and the second half in the Czech University). He also had to address all the scientific associations, for instance the Brentano Association, the Cercle Linguistique, the Cercle Philosophique, the Utitz Seminar, etc. As he was the guest of the Cercle Philosophique, it did not lead to a confrontation with Carnap and the Positivists, for the Cercle was founded in opposition to precisely such unseemliness, and its rules were made accordingly ... (*3.3*)

The text of Husserl's presentation has until now not been reconstructed. Sections of his expositions have undoubtedly been subsumed in his last great work: *Die Krisis der europäischen Wissenschaften und die transzendentale Phänomenologie.* This work appeared in its entirety in Volume VI of the *Husserliana,* but excerpts had already appeared in the first number of the journal *Philosophia,* published by Arthur Liebert in Belgrade in 1936. Similarly, some of the contents of Husserl's Prague address were presumably taken up in the work 'Experience and Judgment' *(Erfahrung und Urteil)* – a work which, significantly, was printed, directly after Husserl's death, in Prague in 1938 as the second of the publications, as planned, of the writings of Prague's *Cercle Philosophique.* However, because the publishing house was closed down as a result of the German annexation of Czechoslovakia, and because the edition (save for 200 copies which found their way to the U.S.A. and England) was subsequently repulped, the book did not appear on the German market until 1948.

Landgrebe annotated Husserl's Prague address – a Czech record of the address (hitherto not translated) is contained in the above-mentioned journal *Slovo a Slovesnost,* Vol. II. The destiny of Husserl's work and the concept of phenomenology were, despite the qualifying remarks of Frau Husserl about mutually opposing points of view, very closely linked to Prague. On 13 May 1938 the *Cercle Philosophique* held a memorial gathering in honour of Husserl, who had been its only honorary member. His pupils, Landgrebe and Patocka, delivered valedictions. Patocka very clearly described the reasons why the connexions with phenomenology were so far-reaching:

Thus the age-old problem of the *a priori* has been tackled anew; no longer, however, in the straight-and-narrow, subjective Kantian form, but as an *a priori* that constitutes the nucleus, the intrinsic structure of realities. In this way the old ontological problem is revived, supplying Husserl's hand with sharpened methodological tools – his method of the *Wesensschau,* of the *eidetische Erfahrung,* which is not concerned with the realities of the here and now but with their inner eternal perspicuity. This method may well be criticized, and has been criticized, but it nevertheless represents concern to attain a fundamentally deeper and more lucid approach to a philosophical awareness of the self than had ever been reached in previous philosophizing. At that time, in almost all disciplines belonging to the cultural sciences, structuralism was experiencing a new boom – one-sided approaches, psychological or sociological, (whether applying to art, religion, or law) were everywhere called into question and supplanted – and this structuralism found its intellectual mainstay in the philosophy of the *Logische Untersuchungen.* In addition, however, entire disciplines that had almost been forgotten excited renewed interest. The problem of a logical grammar was for instance posited anew, thus removing the theory of language from one-sided 'psychologism', the legitimate claims of psychology itself in this field, however, not thereby being overlooked. A series of 'material', abstract, and concrete ontologies came into being. Questions that had not been raised since the days of the Schoolmen and Wolff's school were discussed afresh and new aspects and new conclusions were wrested from them. All modern concerns with a new ontology, even those which belie their origin, have their roots here — in this first phase of Husserl's rediscovery of the idea.

This fragment contains *in nuce* the whole question of the inter-relatedness between phenomenology and structuralism — a problem which has hardly been more sharply and clearly delineated even in present-day philosophical discussions.

Vilèm Mathesius, in the first number of *Slovo a Slovesnost,* described the work of the Prague Circle as a "work symbiosis". In the same number Trubetzkoy called it a "joint accomplishment by researchers bound together by a unity of methodological purpose and inspired by the same guiding principle". We see this in the urbanity of those researches and in their varied perspectives. To this must be reckoned the considerable progress made in the theory of language and in semiotics during the decade from 1916 to 1926. Furthermore, logical positivism developed into an influential philosophical school which, as fundamental study, together with phenomenology and the newer ontology, was capable of breaking the philosophical isolation of formalistic-structuralistic thought. In this regard, and looking back in 1941, the Czech aesthetic and philosopher Jan Mukařovský was to write in his *Kapitel aus der Poetik:*

Currents in science, presaging complete indifference to philosophical questions, are simply surrendering all conscious control over their presuppositions ... Structuralism is neither a *Weltanschauung* that anticipates or oversteps the bounds of empirical data nor is it solely a method (i.e. a series of research techniques that can be applied only to a research field). Preferably, it is a noetic principle which nowadays is carried through in psychology, linguistics, the theory of literature, the theory and history of art, sociology, biology, etc.

With this fundamental observation, the link is forged with the concept (as exposited by Jakobson and Tynjanov in 1928) of a social and aesthetic evolution being a 'system of systems'.

After the Second World War, the climate was not favourable for structuralist thought. Particularly until 1950, the word 'formalism' was a term of abuse, and the position of structuralist researchers resembled that of the formalists in Russia in 1926. Many members of the Prague Circle emigrated. The results of the Copenhagen, New York, and other linguistic circles were limited to a group of Western specialists until such time as, with the generative grammar of Noam Chomsky and with Parisian structuralism, a new florescence of the concept of structuralism may be seen. Vachek has written an outline of the Prague events, in *The Linguistic School of Prague*, 1966, as well as in *A Prague School Reader in Linguistics*, 1964. We may also mention: F.L. Garwin (ed.): *A Prague School Reader in Esthetics, Literary Structure and Style*, 1964; and No. 3 of the Paris journal *Change*, entitled *Le Cercle de Prague*, 1969. E. Benes and J. Vachek, in *Stilistik und Soziolinguistik: Beitrage der Prager Schule zur strukturellen Sprachbetrachtung und Spracherziehung*, 1971, tell us about developments in present-day Czech linguistics which are taking up the inheritance of the Prague School, wishing, however, to develop it further both critically and creatively.

2. CZECH STRUCTURALISM

"Science itself changes — and we change with it." This assertion of Eichenbaum's in his 1925 dissertation *Die Theorie der formalen Methode* might well serve as the theme for analysing the content aspects of Czech structuralism. Eichenbaum summarizes the products of the decade before the founding of the Prague Circle as follows:

(1). Formalism differentiated between the juxtaposition of poetic and practical language, according to the function of language on the one hand and according to regional synchronic language types on the other. In particular, the poetic language, emotional language, and direct and topical speech were penetratingly studied.

(2) The concept of form was viewed in relation to the problems of procedure *(priëm)* and function.

(3) In formalism, rhythm was analysed as example of a constitutional element of language structure, while in the same context dominants were sought in the process of systematizing language. These questions brought the evolution of forms, methods of procedure, and functions all within the same context.

The latter task takes us beyond a limited formalism. The works of Tynjanov (*Das literarische Faktum*, 1928) and of Jakobson and Tynjanov (*Probleme der Sprach- und Literaturforschung*, 1928) provide reasoned evidence of this. Each existence of the self is linked to the development of an idea. Thus the idea of formal method is only to be understood as a development, and thus the principles of the method can only be presented as elements of a general development. Eichenbaum emphasizes that it is precisely here that their scientific nature lies. This latter is characteristic of methodology, not a thing in itself. Eichenbaum concludes:

We do not possess any theory that could be represented as a rounded, closed system. Theory and history for us are amalgamated, not only in the mind but also in practice. We have learned too abundantly from history to think of suppressing history. The moment we admit to ourselves that we possess a theory that explains everything – that can cope with every eventuality of the past and the future, and that neither needs nor is susceptible to evolution – at that moment we shall simultaneously have to admit that the formalistic method has come to the end of the road and that the spirit of scientific research has deserted it.

We mention this significant final deduction because it is not only a conclusion but also points to the future and counters those premature judgments that superficially identify the 'formalistic method' with 'a-historicism'.

In Tynjanov's similarly-disposed investigations, the supposition that a work of art or literature is a *system* plays the leading rôle. This is the epistemological premise upon which scientific research into the aesthetic is based. Literature in particular can accordingly be studied as a succession and systematization of systems. Only in this way do analytical work and experimental constructions become meaningful. The problem is one of *series*; *milieu* becomes literature and literature is subsumed into the *milieu*; periphery becomes the centre; insignificant things turn out to be major interests. These events can only be understood by functional analyses.

Tynjanov and Jakobson's above-mentioned manifesto from the journal *Nowy Lef* brings such points of view under a common denominator. The following main points of the Manifesto illustrate the methodological anacrusis to Czech structuralism:

... it is decidedly necessary to free oneself from academic eclecticism and from scholastic 'formalism' which seek to replace analysis with no more than the naming and the cataloguing of phenomena; and from repeated attempts to pervert the theory of language and literature from a systematic science into episodic and anecdotal genres.

The theory of literature and of art, respectively, narrowly linked to other historical disciplines, are characterized, like each of these fields, by a multi-layered complex of specific structural laws. If the legitimacy of these laws is not made clear, it is impossible to emply scientific criteria to determine the interacting relationship between literary achievement and other historical disciplines.

... The material used in literature, whether itself drawn from literary or non-literary sources, can only be made available to scientific inquiry if it is examined in terms of its function at the time.

... Today, however, the findings of a synchronic approach compel us to examine anew the principles of diachronism. The presentation of a mechanical agglomeration of phenomena, which would, in the domain of synchronic inquiry, be replaced by the concepts of system and structure, would also, in the domain of diachronic inquiry, be decisively supplanted. The history of a system in itself creates a system. Pure synchrony now appears illusory; every synchronic system contains its past and its future as an indivisible structural element of its own system ... .

Analysis of the structural laws of language and literature and their evolution leads unavoidably to a finite series of actual, given types of structure — types of structural development for that matter.

... The revelation of immanent legitimacies in literature and the history of language respectively makes it possible to depict every concrete change in literary as well as in language systems. On the other hand, it is not possible to foretell the rate of evolution nor the direction which the development will choose to take from among those theoretically possible ... This question can only be solved by means of an analysis of the correlation between literature and the other historical disciplines. The reciprocal relationship (a system of systems) has its own structural laws that should be studied. To examine the correlation of the systems without reference to the immanent laws that are unique to each system would be disastrous. (*2.16*, 74ff.)

In connexion with the questions we have posed, the following points emerge.

(a) The foregoing theses clearly indicate a retreat from pure formalism. Insight into the complexity of aesthetic facts has grown; the requirement of legitimacy where structure is concerned ought to deal with the initial (and in any case understandable) despair at such complexities. Legitimacy as such rests primarily upon epistemological intervention, consisting of functional and structural analysis. This intervention should take the place of the usual genetic procedures, and their concomitant tradition of understanding and interpretation.

(b) In addition, an attempt should be made, in studying the evolution of the structural laws of literature and language, to apply the distinction that dates back to Baudoiun de Courtenay in 1870 — the distinction between *jazyk* and *reč*; De Saussure expressed this distinction by using the words *langue* and *parole*. Nowadays, we speak of *code* and *message*, or of *competence* and *performance*. In this way, the diachronic aspect of the synchronic are also studied.

(c) If we are critical, we must doubt whether, either in these arguments or in the works accompanying them, the hoped-for legitimacies have actually been achieved. This is what distinguishes these Theses from the Manifesto of the Prague Circle in 1929. The concepts 'structure' and 'system' are used indiscrimately — a fact which, as we have already mentioned in the first chapter, is still characteristic of discussions today.

(d) Finally, it has not been clearly stated how a structuralistic hermeneutics is to be grasped, nor how structuralist insights are to be concretely developed. These problems were first taken up by the Czech structuralists, particulary in the disquisitions of the philosopher and aesthetic Jan Mukařovský.

A. *The Prague Theses*

The theses of the Prague Circle join the trains of thought developed by Tynjanov and Jakobson. In the first place, they should be thought of as a complete programme of structuralist thought. At the same time, however, they were a contribution to the Slavistic Congress of the time. Thus in the first three paragraphs we primarily find theoretical expositions of the structural approach, while paragraphs 4 to 9 mainly illustrate applications to the special problems of Slavistics.

In the first section, written by Jakobson, language is presented as a functional system. The explicative character of the intentionality of the speaking subject necessitates a functional approach. Seen thus, language appears as a system of means of expression, functioning all the time with respect to a goal. This goal is not necessarily a communicative one. Thus, one cannot understand any linguistic fact without at the same time developing an understanding of the system, and by so doing the relevant language appears more real.

This approach brings us directly to a number of fundamentals that are typical of the development of structuralist thought. In the first place, we find the problems of synchrony and diachrony here too. The material of language is in fact part and parcel of the same life complex. A synchronic analysis of such material is indeed the only possible way of getting to know the nature and character of the relevant language. The specific attributes of a particular language ought therefore to be catalogued and synchronically analysed. But we need to cross the boundary drawn by the Geneva School: the diachronic does not exclude study of function and system. On the contrary, without such study the diachronic perspective is incomplete just as the synchronic cannot manage without the diachronic.

In the second place, fresh light is shed on the chances of a comparative treatment of linguistics. In the new as against the traditional method, not only may specific language complexes and their social and historical materials henceforth be compared with one another, but structural laws of linguistic systems may also be discovered and compared — diachronically as well as synchronically. Both the convergent and the divergent are thus elucidated. The convergent, in the light of comparative structural treatment, seems to appear divergent; whereas the divergent suddenly stands revealed as convergent. We thus overcome what has for the most part been a fictitious and often sterile method, i.e. of viewing historical facts and contemporaneous tendencies in isolation, or, at best, as the results of a hidden mechanism.

In the second section, also formulated by Jakobson, the structural principle of the phonological system is outlined. The fundamental task in analysing the system is the search for constituent elements, i.e. for phonemes, for phonological correlations with the language system, and for the ordering or various groups of phonemes. These are all elements of a phonological and morphological description of the structure of language.

The same procedure holds for words. When a word is looked at according to its function, it is taken as the result of a denominative activity — all mechanistic ways of regarding a language then become possible. Jakobson finds the autonomous existence of a word selfevident, manifesting itself to varying degrees in various languages. This 'naming activity' enables language to analyse reality into accessible linguistic entities, regardless of whether reality is external or internal, concrete or abstract. The old 'representation theory' is abandoned, and replaced by one that is analytic and at the same time constructive.

Every language has its own specific system of denomination, which, because it is systemic, allows us to think of supplementing the traditional syntax-bound study of words by a comprehensive functional system. We thus arrive at the following construction. A word is the result of a linguistic denomination; a grouping of words is the result of a syntaxmatic procedure (i.e. the outcome of a study of the complex entity of the relevant language signs, such as words); the fundamental function of this syntaxmatic procedure is predicative. The way the subject functions linguistically becomes clear only by studying predicative activity in the language. Starting in this way, complex language events, ordinarily classified as poetic, practical, or emotional speech, may be analysed and reduced to a common structural.

This is what the third paragraph of the Prague thesis is about. Two distinctions play an important rôle here. Language that is latent in the mind is different from that which is manifested in speech. Similarly we have the further distinction, analysed in formalist studies, between 'practical' and 'poetical' language.

The first distinction is philosophically interesting, and is also to be found in present-day structuralism. The majority of speaking subjects, says Jakobson, regard the language they use in speaking as a particular case, because "they apply linguistic forms in thinking more often than in speaking." In other words, linguistic forms exist as internal forms, as internalized forms that are made real by speaking. Both speaking and thinking are thus the realization of internalized forms of language. The traditional distinction between the conscious and the un- or sub-conscious therefore no longer concerns us. The internalization of speech forms can only take place by speaking and thinking. Living as we do in a world in which speech is used, we throughout our lives internalize linguistic forms. Putting these into use occupies no more

than a few moments of the total internalization process. On the other hand,
putting language to use is not an optional action; it has to take place so that
the process of internalization may be carried out.

About the second distinction, it is interesting to note that functional analysis of practical and literary language is not much more successful than that
of poetical language. Even in formalism one comes across this fact. We need
not wonder at this, because the autonomy of poetical language is clearly
recognizable. The way the phonological acts as a model — very characteristic
of the Prague approach — is clearer when applied to poetical language. Even
the material content of poetical language is more amenable to phonological
analysis than that of practical language.

In the foregoing analyses, Jakobson and Mukařovský start from the fact
that historians of literature, while certainly concerning themselves with poetic
language, have not at the same time kept its independent character sufficiently
clearly in mind. Therefore, we should now first undertake a synchronic analysis. Traces of an individual creative action as found in poetic language are,
however, derived from a poetic tradition as well as from the language of practical communication. This very interconnexion should also be studied synchronically, but at the same time not overlooking the wider context that
would include diachronic study as well. Only when based upon these double
axes will the unity of poetic language emerge, and can it be taken as the
point of departure of the analysis. Because of this unity, the traditional procedure in the theory of literature (in which the phonological, morphological,
diachronic, and other aspects of poetic language used to be studied separa-
tely) is no longer practicable. The fundamental principle remains, i.e. that
"poetical work forms a functional structure, and its different elements may
not be understood outside of its unified framework."

Especially in poetry, however, it becomes apparent that the same elements
function differently in different combinations. The formalistic treatment of
alienation serves to increase the diversity of these functions, and thus to
emphasize the systemic character of what is poetical. As a result, the poetic
elements of language need to be seen as part of a predetermined scheme of
values. This makes the autonomy of the poetical clear and brings its characteristic property to the fore. All elements of language that play a subservient
rôle in exclusively communicative language achieve, in poetical language, a
value in their own right. In putting poetic language into practice, the automatic hierarchy of language elements is abandoned, and a poetic semantics
that can stand on its own results.

B. *Art as a Sign*

The principles of developing structuralist thought may be discerned from the excerpts of the Prague theses discussed here. The works of the philosopher and aesthete, Jan Mukařovský, clearly elaborate these principles. Important points in his discussion are: (i) art as a semiological fact; (ii) the rôle of the subject in functionalist thought; (iii) the specificity of the aesthetic function and definition of other functions.

(i) Art is a semiological fact. Structuralist aesthetics may in this sense be viewed as part of a general study of signs. Formalism, phonology, and structural linguistics give rise to this point of view; sociological and psychological analyses must be seen in this perspective. We are no longer concerned (as Jakobson and Tynjanov were) solely with literature, or the theory of literature, but with aesthetics as such. The statement that all that is aesthetic is like a sign does not rest merely upon a statement about art as a fact on its own. It is equally concerned with the creator, the so-called 'subjectivity' of the artist, the inner structure of the work of art as much as with the relationship between art and society. The bold venture of taking a good look at and then getting a grip on this complex is characteristic of Czech structuralism. Mukařovský, in his address to the Philosophical Congress in Prague in 1934, enjoined his audience to bear in mind that:

the problems of sign and meaning become increasingly pressing because all spiritual content that exceeds the bounds of individual consciousness, from the sheer fact of its communicability, acquires the character of a sign. The science of signs (semiology to de Saussure, sematology to Bühler, must be explored in all its breadth. Just as contemporary linguistics (for instance, the researches of the Prague School, i.e. the Prague Linguistic Circle) expands the field of semantics, so the insights of semantic linguistics should be applied to all other types of signs, differentiated according to their special features. Indeed, there is a whole group of sciences specially interested in questions concerning signs (as also in problems of structure, and value, which are after all closely associated with problems concerning signs – a work of art is for instance at the same time sign, structure, and value). These are the *Geisteswissenschaften* (*sciences morales*), dealing with material which, to a greater or lesser extent has the explicit character of a sign, which explains their twofold existence – in the world of the senses and in collective (or social) consciousness. (*3.5*, 138)

The methodological principle here is functionalistic. It renders an analysis which, within one general framework, examines both the specificity of the aesthetic and its societal content.

Mukařovský derives his functional analysis, as applied to the relationship between art and society, in the first place from the Marxist theory of the 'Widerspiegelung'. He emphasizes that the development of artistic structure is continuous and characterized by internal legitimacy; it is self-motivated. We

should thus regard art as more than merely a direct result of social developments. It is true that changes in the artistic structure are prompted from outside, but the nature and the direction in which such impulses are perceived and
developed depend solely upon immanent aesthetic presuppositions. These
aesthetic presuppositions do not necessarily bring about a causal-mechanical
relationship between art and society, just as a given form of social organization does not necessarily carry with it a corresponding form of artistic creation. The reason why there is no fixed mechanism lies in the artist himself.
He as it were forges the link between art and society because he belongs not
only to the creative process but also to the current form of society. This
doesn't at all imply an invariable and essential synchronism between artist
and public; it merely emphasizes the fact that in the process of artistic creation the public, the *other,* is always in some way present. This achieves for
us a new approach to the problem of subjectivity of the artist. A work of art
is no longer one-sidedly dependent on its creator. Consequently, it is able
because of this to view the problem of individuality realistically. The analysis being made here in relation to aesthetics may well have general philosophical and anthropological consequences. The structural-functional way of looking at the relationship between individual and society makes it clear, where
human creativity is concerned, that a more flexible view of the link between
the creator and his product is necessary if the role of the creator in a societal
context is to be correctly interpreted. This flexibility is acceptable if we
regard a work of art as a sign, not only in relation to the individual but
also to the society.

When we assess a work of art as a token, we destroy the mechanical
model of the 'Widerspiegelung'. This supports the view that an aesthetic object
ought to be thought of as a whole. Only as a whole can it fulfil its function
as a sign, and only as a whole can it be understood societally. Despite much
change in the relationship of art and society — a demonstrable historical
fact — every societal development has a holistic understanding of artistic
structure as a whole. The artistic currents in previous centuries imply this in
all their nomenclatures — in concepts such as realism, expressionism, symbolism, cubism, etc. These in fact, as concepts of a particular artistic structure, remain valid within markedly differing organizational forms of society.
We have only to remind ourselves of the fact, already referred to, that
cubism appeared simultaneously in Russia and in France, and was based
upon similar aesthetic and philosophical principles, although the societal
structures of the two countries were at the time very dissimilar. A given
societal structure can come to understand works of art that were created in
a quite different, or in an earlier, societal structure. Indeed, such works are

often better understood than by their own contemporaries. In other words, a society basically has all works of art at its disposal — from its own past and the past of others, from its own present and the present of others — that are able relevantly to express certain insights and interpretations. Thus Mukařovský's accomplishments seem to anticipate Malraux's idea of a *musée imaginaire*. This fact cannot be explained unless we remember to think of art as a sign. The inevitability which a mechanistic model implies in the relationship between society and art does not affect the manner and form of expression, but only the fact that the two are interdependent. Mukařovský says that "the society wants art to lend its expression, and on the other hand art wants to try out its influence on social events". Or, to quote an expression of Baudelaire's: "Society, which passionately loves its counterfeit, also loves (and by no means only half-heartedly) the artist, to whom it entrusts its representation." This purpose is neither individual nor merely social; it is neither idealistically nor mechanistically explained in the 'Widerspiegelung' theory. Perhaps it is to be analysed functionally and to be understood structurally.

The semiological nature of art contradicts all these theories. Other consequences, however, follow from this view of how art originates. In the first place, we should note that a work of art cannot be identified with the state of mind of its creator, nor with that of its recipient. Being an independent and material fact, it is intended as mediator between creator and receiver. Nevertheless, it is not wholly material. The appearance and the inner structure of a work of art changes in time and space, also when it is made public within its social context. Mukařovský cites as example a successive series of translations of works of poetry. "The material work here has the status only of an outward symbol (*signifiant*, in de Saussure's terminology) which promises a particular meaning in the collective consciousness ... and which is determined by those subjective conscious circumstances which members of a given group have in common and which are evoked by the material work." To these must be added subjective psychic elements, and associative factors (Fechner) — these after all are subjective elements which, according to the place of art in the community, give rise to other structures. They bring more objective features to the fore when a classical work is being considered than would be the case with a cubist or a surrealist work. It should be stressed that here too we are concerned not only with the objective structure of the relevant work of art but equally with the (social) structure in which it is received. Until recently, aesthetics (particularly under the influence of idealistic philosophers) was only aesthetics of production. The functional and structural approach has surmounted this, so

that to what had been an aesthetics of production has been added components derived from the recipients. This once again raises the question of the
constitutive rôle of subjectivity — only in terms of a functionalist theory
can the subjectivity of the recipient attain objective semiological value. (2.7)

When considering the characteristics of art as a sign, we must bear in mind
that, while every work of art can indeed be described as an autonomous sign
acting as mediator between the members of a collective (this refers to the
specificity of the aesthetic function), its qualities are nevertheless determined
by two spheres of reality. One is the reality of the sign itself, and the other
is the reality of what it describes — these two together constitute that particular
sign, which we generally call 'art'. This autonomy of the sign indicates that the
intended meaning is something lying within the understanding that is shared
between sender and receiver. This 'something' is the whole context that en-
compasses certain social phenomena (such as philosophy, politics, science,
etc.) from a specific societal structure. The link between the sign 'art' and
this social context can be close or loose — many structural relations are possible. Once again we see that a mechanistic theory doesn't hold; only a semio-
logical-functionalist theory can provide us with insight into the interconnexions between art and society.

The sign function is thus not sufficiently explained merely by referring
to autonomy. The function of communication must be added to it. This
becomes particularly clear in the so-called 'thematic arts'. The symbol
itself does not change its nature, the meaning is still conveyed by the whole
aesthetic object, but a particular one from among all of the components of
the work of art is highlighted, to become the theme of the work. As with
the purely communicative sign, we now find that the relationship to the
thing portrayed suggests something that has an identifiable existence — Mukařovský points to components such as event, *Gestalt,* thing, etc. But the
relationship between the work of art and the thing portrayed has no existential value, which is an important difference, when compared with the
purely communicative sign. A work of art as a whole *has* existential value
— the substance makes up only one of the components of the whole. This
component however, especially conveys that aspect of the whole semiological nature that is the communicative one. Thus a duality is created in the
nature of a work of art as a sign which is unavoidable, and is very differently
expressed in the various arts. When the functionalist semiological approach
is used, it appears as a universal and homogeneous problem.

(ii) The semiological approach, as has been shown above, casts new light upon
the rôle of the subject in art. Mukařovský takes as his point of departure the

assertion; "The 'I', the *subject*, which appears in every art and in every work in some or other guise (though the guise may differ a great deal), is identified neither with any concrete, psychosomatic individual, nor with the author. The whole artistic structure of the work concentrates on this point, and is ordered according to it. Nevertheless, any personality can be projected upon it — that of an author as well as that of a receiver." (*3.4*, 16)

This apparently lapidary sentence serves boldly to contrast structuralistic aesthetics with the philosophical tradition of idealism. Since it was written, the *décentrement* of the subject has become the core of the structuralistic debate. The fundamentally idealistic concept of a subject as an autonomous and authoritarian point of orientation for all events is abandoned, and a polyfunctional concept adopted instead. The aesthetic may once more serve as example. Here, the question of the individuality of the author is much less interesting than the question of how individuality functions as a factor in artistic work. Not only the author is such a factor. The individuality of the recipients (patrons or commissioners of work of art, or even publishers, critics, and art dealers) is of equal importance. Groups such as artistic schools or movements may also take on the same individualizing function, for a generation or for a more-or-less homogeneous public.

Thus a new philosophical conception arises from psychological and socio-logical approaches. Precise questions arise — questions which no longer con-fine themselves to aesthetics but may be generalized to include philosophi-cal inquiries of the greatest significance. Is man to be seen as author of his works and deeds? Is he master of those events and relationships which he seems himself to have called into being? Does his presumed creativity mani-fest the individual freedom which we rate so high as to think of it as the essence of his existence, or is our conclusion specious and of an ideological nature? The structuralist approach abandons this authorship in favour of a functionalist interpretation. Man as a product of some or other ideal including man as an outcome of his own wishes and ideals is recognized as a latent ideological factor. In this light, his reality is seen as a broken perspective, Individual human existence (a late manifestation in Occidental thought) i.e. man's existence as an authentic and authoritarian being, becomes relative. Instead, a freely determinable individuality is conjured up. *Décentrement* has a liberating effect, even when it cannot be separated from the functional framework. After all, freedom is always only possible in terms of an ordered structure, otherwise it becomes the absurdity of a freedom in the pitiless desert.

Intentions and their outcomes just do not produce such unbroken and inevitably linked chains as past anthropological value-systems enjoin us to forge. We must recognize that intentions and outcomes may become disconnected. When we say that our intentions have been fulfilled, are they still *our* intentions, or does the result immediately appear as part of an almost limitless complex of actions, in the face of which the question of authorship becomes an absurdity? Man is never an individual; he is much more of a singularized universal. Being continuously singularized by birth and lifetime, he endows this singularization with a name — this name is then recognized as a provisional arrangement and a sign. This recognition is accomplished particularly in *dialogue*. Significantly, this form of speech, as a topical application of the 'sign' of language, appears in Czech structuralism, especially in a work of Mukařovský's on the dialogue (1940). How Mukařovský treated his subject illustrates how closely linguistic and anthropological questions meet. They are linked in a study of Gabriel Tarde's, *L'opinion et la foule*, 1922, and with a linguistic work of L.P. Jakubinskij, *O, dialogičeskoj reči*, 1923. Where earlier conceptions suggested that the choice between monologue and dialogue was random and linguistically irrelevant, being solely a by-product of the use of language as a sign, Jakubinskij included dialogue and monologue among the functional languages. He showed that the application of one or the other is a linguistic act of choice between two fixed and legitimate complexes of conventions in speech. Further doubt about the rôle of the subject, however, immediately arises here — the aforesaid choice is on occasion made by the speaking individual. This choice, however, does not depend solely on the intention of that individual. The speaking individual cannot take in all the implications of his choice, and probably not even one consciously knows which choice he makes in speaking. The reality of such choice is, however, not solipsistic — it is jointly determined by the companion in speech. Thus the monologue character of a dialogue and dialogue character of a monologue depend on the speakers, who not only do not have unfettered control over the share of the other at times, but equally little over the conventionality of the form of speaking in which they find themselves. So monologue and dialogue are elementary (if not entirely existential) attitudes, which link the way of speaking with the reality that exists outside language.

Mukařovský now points to some of the main features of the dialogue. In the first place, the designation of an 'I' or a 'you' can only be grasped functionalistically. "The polarity between the I and the you is so evident in dialogue that in this polarity the rôles of the speaker and the listener are continuously changing. The mutual relationship of the partners to the conversation is experienced as tension which cannot be pinned onto any one of the two speakers, but really exists 'between' them ..." (*3.4*, 115) The history of the constitution of the conversation is accordingly not to be found in the intentionality of the speakers of the time. The speaking subjects are 'decentralized' and a 'between' actually exists between them. The constitutive power of this 'betweenness' becomes a fundamental element in the so-called philosophy of dialogue, as developed by Ebner, Rosenzweig, and Buber. In this philosophy too the *décentrement* of the subjects is a pre-requisite for revealing the structure of the conversation. At this point, structuralism and dialogal philosophy come into contact with one another, and a common anthropological denominator appears.

Secondly, the nature of the situation should be brought out. The more or less objective situation, which becomes an element of the total speech situation dialogue and surrounds it, can come into the conversation both directly and indirectly. The fact that such a situation is present can occupy the foreground — it can also be kept altogether in the background. Nevertheless, it is always there and equally deprives the speaker of power. Even when we 'discuss a situation', we don't really discuss the situation in which we find ourselves speaking; it joins in the talk while being talked about.

Thirdly, we should consider the nature of the semantic structure. This lands us in the centre of the verbalization itself. Other than in monologue, utterances in dialogue penetrate the self, and distinguish it from at least two, perhaps even more contexts, which can reach semantic unity only in dialogue. This unity is provided by the theme. The penetrating, often the opposing, nature of the contexts in dialogue causes marked changes of direction which are very valuable when analysing dialogue functionally. The way in which the 'I' and the 'you' are context-bonded, and the marked changes in the factuality of an 'I' and a 'you' that are limited by time, become very clear in dialogue. The principles, according to which, functionally and semiologically, the motives for individualizing (respectively indicated by 'I' and 'you') operate, are so clear in dialogue that one is inclined to take them as a model for the interpretation of subjectivity. The dialogue possesses a tendency towards maximal and uninterrupted semantic variability; a variability which holds good for actual dialogue as well as for the so-called 'inner monologue' (Dujardin). Would one be inclined, on these grounds (i.e., in the last analysis, because of the close interconnexions between speech and thought), to pronounce this variability to be a variability of subject?

(iii) Such questionings are very closely connected with the problem of the specificity of the aesthetic function. Although there are artists, and one keeps on maintaining that they create works of art, it is nevertheless clear that the aesthetic function is based on things that are not wholly within the power of the individual. This is true, not only because the aesthetic is neither a real attribute of things, nor bound in a way that has only one meaning to particular attributes of things, but it proves true also because aesthetic judgment and aesthetic effect are intersubjective events; and, in a work of art, one is not sure whether it is indeed they which contain the very essence of what makes it a work of art. Because the first impact of the work of art, the experience of its aesthetic effect, is hardly affected by aesthetic judgment upon it. The work of art which 'says something' to me, operates within the framework of my world; it is subsumed in the framework without, however, determining it. When the work of art says something to me, it speaks to me when I am listening, and not when I am myself speaking.

This is the linguistic dimension in which the problem of the aesthetic function lies. The subject of the discussion no longer is whether beauty exists independently of man, but concerns the aesthetic in the human frame of action. Therefore structuralist aesthetics may be clearly distinguished from idealistic aesthetics. To quote Mukařovský's words in an address in 1942: "As fundamental methodological premise, the concept of function takes the place of the concept of beauty: human creations, as concrete actions from which human activity is built up, take the place of natural phenomena." (*3.4*, 115) Roland Barthes viewed technique as the essence of human creativity; Mukařovský also draws a clear line between nature and art.

The functional approach reinstates a reciprocal relationship between the aesthetic that is external and the aesthetic that is internal to art, and examines its transitions and its other relationships. The aesthetic problem is thus reduced to an anthropological level, as was the case with Cassirer and other thinkers influenced by semiotics. Since no human activity is without the aesthetic function to be present, we must accept the aesthetic as an element of human action and human *Gestalt*. Clearly, wheresoever in art the aesthetic function fundamentally dominates, extra-aesthetic functions also play a part. The sphere of art thus conforms to the general rule that human action is fundamentally diversified, and fundamentally ubiquitous.

In addition, it is necessary to distinguish structural functionalism from earlier forms of functionalism. Both presuppose that a predominating, strictly limited function exists. Using architectural functionalism as an example, it would be clear from the outset what the function of a building would be. This makes of such architecture a typical monistic product, and leads to clearly demarcated value judgments. But, just as a building is not created by its function, so all human states of affairs are polyfunctional and polyvalent. In other words, they cannot be one-sidedly projected onto the object, but all find their grounding in the subject. Therefore, as soon as we, as Mukařovský suggests, "look at the functions with the eyes of the subject, we recognize that every action, with which man directs himself to reality so as to react upon it in some or other way, corresponds simultaneously and unavoidably to several purposes which the individual himself (from whom the action springs) has hitherto not been able to tell apart." As long as one views the function from the vantage of the object, it appears to be bound to a particular purpose, to given value criteria; monofunctionalist interpretations result. Structural functionalism, on the other hand, looks at function from the changing vantage of the relevant subject in a way that makes the subject realize itself in relation to the outer world. Polyfunctionalism results. This way of looking at things can contribute to the systemic character of structuralist thought.

The functionalism of structuralist thought is thus fundamentally polyfunctional. This has implications for the wider definition of the aesthetic function, and also for the analysis of the more general principles of functionalism in structuralism.

The analysis of the specificity of such aesthetic function – Mukařovský speaks of a phenomenological analysis that leaves genetic questions out of account – starts from the fact that there are two ways for man to realize himself in relation to reality: via direct and via signal functions. The direct function is either practical or theoretical. In the practical function the object is in the foreground because we are here concerned with the metamorphosis of the object. In the theoretical function, the subject is in the foreground because the goal is to define the projection of reality in the consciousness of the subject (indeed, in a form unified according to the singularity of the subject). Reality itself· remains untouched in this projected model.

The signal functions, too, may be dichotomised. When the object comes to the fore, we speak of the symbolic function – what counts here is how effective the relation is between what is being symbolized and the sign that is used to symbolize. When the subject comes to the fore, we speak of the aesthetic function. All that this function (as it were) lays hands on it changes into signs. Whereas the connexion between the subject and the symbolic function bears upon individual realities, this connexion in the case of the aesthetic function bears upon reality as a whole. We thus arrive again at a mirror theory. If reality as a whole is mirrored by the aesthetic sign (an interpretation Mukařovský advocated in 1942), the model of a mirror is after all structuralistic, i.e. polyfunctional and not mechanistic-deterministic. The following diagram serves as illustration:

$$
\text{Function}
\begin{cases}
\text{direct}
\begin{cases}
\text{practical : object focussed / metamorphous} \\
\\
\text{theoretical : subject focussed / projective}
\end{cases} \\
\\
\text{signal}
\begin{cases}
\text{symbolic : object focussed / effective} \\
\\
\text{aesthetic : subject focussed / signifying}
\end{cases}
\end{cases}
$$

The aesthetic function reminds us of the theoretical function. The latter however concerns a unified *picture* of reality, whereas the aesthetic function brings about a unifying *way of relating to* reality.

Further analyses flow from the fact that we can only differentiate the practical functions. We are left with the need that is characteristic for structural thought, to trace the correlations of the various functions in a differentializing way. The typology knows no sub- or super-ordering. The principle of structuralism (which leads us to see hierarchies as dynamic processes) gives rise to a structural analysis in which, in the case of structural aesthetics as designed by Mukařovský, the aesthetic function appears as the point of departure in the analysis of the polyfunctional.

C. *Functionalism and Structuralism*

Czech structuralism, particularly in the theories here presented, bears a decidedly functionalist stamp, a general legacy from biology. Organic life, it seemed, has been pinned down by values based upon description. The organism was thus no longer conceived of as a being with a soul but as an adaptive system reacting meaningfully, by its own doing, upon changing environmental circumstances. The goal of its reactions was to maintain structural homeostasis as far as possible. How far the system reacts upon influences, mobilizes its defences, and with what mechanisms it preserves stability are additional important questions. This way of thinking seems to promise that homeostasis will be maintained, although it represents no more than a model of life-processes. The capacity (also attributed to living creatures) to keep their 'internal' *milieu* (i.e. a particular condition) unimpaired despite manifold internal and external disturbances has been called *ultrastability* by Ross Ashby, who discovered it. Ultrastable systems can stabilize their systems by adaptation and by exercising choice (or spontaneity), both of which are important characteristics of life. This process is explained by the principle of moving stages. The system, in maintaining stability, transfers from one field of variables to another – it can even happen that an ultrastable system abandons all areas which could transpose it into critical (i.e. unstable) conditions and retains those in which a stable condition can be achieved (*5.1,* 91). This example aids our biological understanding of adaptation of organisms to variable environmental circumstances.

When the theory is applied to social organizations, however, its value orientations are no longer purely descriptive. A functionalist theory of social systems results, in which they are thought of as a functional complex of institutions. These institutions are made up of rôles and norms that combine and are binding upon groups and individuals. Cultural values are steering mechanisms determining the degree of integration and the measure of stability of the social system. Functionalism and structuralism thus appear as complementary theories: functionalist theory studies the relevant system empirically, while structuralist theory studies the differential correspondences and deviations of the various functional systems. Both are subject, however, to similar criticism: they tend to control social practice *via* the regulatory mechanism mentioned here, or at least to provide the means for such manipulative control. Adaption, co-operation, conformity, functionality, all appear now as fundamental concepts of a controlled social stability which, as immanent value in the system, continues to be sought. What is overlooked is that stability acts here as a value-bonded problem which, in relation to a continuously changing environment, does not represent reality but, on the contrary, creates it.

Such criticism seems justified when we recall Foucault's assertion with which we ended our first chapter: "The endeavour, at present undertaken by some of our generation is ... to show that our thinking, our lives, our way of being, right down to the details of our day-to-day behaviour, are all part and parcel of the same organizational scheme; consequently they depend upon the same categories as do the scientific and technical universe." (*0.8,* 9.4) Is the above-mentioned criticism actually justified?

We should immediately ask ourselves whether Mukařovský's idea of polyfunctionalism might accord with this criticism. Lucien Goldmann escapes such criticism in so far as the structuralism he has developed is a genetic one. Foucault points out that current humanistic anthropology is abstract and bound to ideology, which is the basis of criticism of this kind.

The foundation of the theory of polyfunctionalism is that there are no spheres of human action exclusively restricted, irrevocably and existentially, to *one* function. Other functions always appear — often such as were not thought of by the author or the producer, or not desired by him. Functional relativism governs the world of human action. Functionalism, understood in this sense, tries to understand the truth that human action, always function-bonded, is ultimately indeterminate. It rests upon the insight that every action in which man addresses himself to reality fulfils several purposes often indistinguishable even to the individual himself. Limitation of function, and the requirement that function be determinable, are *social* desiderata. A linguistic model might possibly help us to understand them — as manifestations of a determining social value-structure. Thus the reproaches listed here do not apply to functionalism as such, but are relevant only when functionalism is applied in a way predetermined by particular values.

Goldmann's genetic structuralism would immediately oppose a dogmatic functionalist application of structural thought. With such an application, the problems mentioned above would indeed be valid. Nevertheless, genetic structuralism does proceed from the fact that all people try to link their thought, experience, and demeanour to a meaningful and coherent structure. In addition, it is always necessary to orient oneself to a group, or to a small number of groups. Thus the functionalist approach does not create a world that consists of nothing more than adjustment, but instead tries to prevent an ostrich-like ideology of 'freedom' from obscuring the empirically obvious need for structuring. Fundamental anthropological facts, such as the tendency to adapt oneself to the environment and to orient oneself towards it meaningfully and rationally (in other words, the tendency towards something akin to coherence and structure), and the dynamics of these facts, are thus brought into central focus.

Both these theses do not impute any value to human behaviour; they merely try to describe and understand actual behaviour and thus to discover hitherto neglected processes. This is not pure description in the classical sense — a structure cannot without more ado be extracted from the so-called 'concrete' reality. A linguistic model makes the constructional character of the description clear — it doesn't concern the flow of the spoken language, but concerns grammar and syntax. Only then does comparison become possible, and true insight into the dynamics of the processes. Moreover, the differential principle inherent in linguistics is retained. We are concerned, not with analysis of fixed structures, but rather with differences between certain open systems of relationship — not with the symmetries, but with the conflicts that make up the history of human action. In this connexion, Foucault notes that humanism, which opposes such a functionalist point of view, is itself an abstraction and an ideology. "All these cries from the heart, these claims made for the human person and human existence, are abstract, i.e. cut off from the scientific and technical world that is, after all, our real world. What makes me oppose humanism is because it is the screen behind which reactionary thought hides, and behind which monstrous and inconceivable alliances are made." (*0.8*, 94)

Foucault is, however, here not advocating a study that is 'value-free'. He, for instance, regards it as his task to make syntheses independent of ideologies and of mechanisms that steer one towards particular values. "We, however, strive to link man to his science, to his discoveries, and to his concrete world." Such linking could have as its goal a conception of man as a concrete totality, thus allowing him to be the 'authentic person' that he is.

D. *Synopsis and Future Prospects*

Czech structuralism brought structural thought to its full flower. This is apparent from the fact that it knew how to free itself from dogmatic formalism. Furthermore, we see a retreat from a point of view that is bound solely to the theory of language and literature, without, however, thereby jeopardizing the function of the linguistic model. Next, we see how this model applies to aesthetics and later to more complex questions concerning social reality. Sociological and social-psychological observations and questions are particularly evident in Czech structuralism. We also find that this structuralism develops a consequent polyfunctionalism, retaining the linguistic differentialism of the Geneva School as a methodological principle. In addition, we see in the thirties the influence of phonology, linguistics, and the theory of literature. In like measure, we see the influence of mathematics, physics, and biology. Clearly, a 'natural' language no longer suffices to convey concepts and suppositions initiated by the natural and the cultural sciences when considering the relationship between man and reality. The technico-constructive character of the concept 'structure' itself is an example of this. New concepts are meaningful only in relation to the theory as a whole. In turn, the extent of the relevant theories that oppose it can only be understood if the theory is looked at as a whole. Czech structuralism demonstrates that more is at issue than merely the immediate application of those concepts to a concrete, perceptible reality. Abstract relationships and theoretical (i.e. constructed) entities become objects of study: theory explains and understands theory. Relationships elucidate the nature of other relationships — a self-supportive world of new comprehensibles comes into being. The requirement, imposed by the philosophy of positivism, that only such concepts as could be related directly or indirectly to sense-data are permissible, and positivism's preference for definitive pronouncements within the domain of 'natural' language, alike become meaningless. Scientific pronouncements are formulated as hypotheses — the results of a construction. Phenomenology influenced the development of Czech structuralism especially in so far as it sought to rehabilitate the general, the ideal, and (linked with these) the attempt to explain the nature of those aspects of reality that we take as 'given'. The features of reality that clearly seem to be individual hypotheses, predetermined and independent of any embodiment, are shown to be general, ideational, and often formal. Husserl's attempt at phenomenology was thus ontologically experienced. His view of existence, 'eidetic' experience, and all other considerations aiming at this ontological apriority, can only be understood within the context of transcendental phenomenology. Looking at the phenomenological development as a whole, such philosophical concepts of self-consciousness become clear — the concept of an ideal structure is seen to be the first step towards understanding the notion of a universal, irresistible totality.

If we turn to the themes of Czech structuralism, we are struck by its connexions with philosophical tradition. Increasing complexity in the fundamental demands made by neo-positivism, i.e. in phenomenological and socio-philosophical problems, support the structuralist approach. The elucidation of the structure of dialogue, particularly via analyses of poetry and drama, call for special attention. This elucidation had a fixed point of departure — the idea of the semiological. It was hoped that this would make new approaches possible — a relative approach would lay all the ghosts of Marxist, idealistic, and other philosophical presuppositions. The specificity of human creativity was recognized as a technique, and the boundaries with reality that are created by human action were clearly brought out. When one bases one's thought on the ways in which man realizes himself vis-à-vis external reality, traditional approaches fall away. Priorities accorded to the aesthetic, to the practical or the theoretical, or to individual awarenesses, give way to a more comprehensive view of human activity. Of special interest is the central position of the subject favoured by our culture — a theme that has become the nub of the debate — viz. the decentralization of the subject. The polemic with idealism and Marxism has been kept alive by this theme and this methodology, which characterize Czech structuralism as well as the work of the Prague School, and make differences with the Copenhagen School and with American approaches apparent. In Copenhagen, language was conceived of chiefly as an algebraic structure with a mathematical theory as background promising the empiric principles of incontrovertibility, completeness, and simplicity. American streams of structural thought on the other hand arose out of ethnolinguistics with psychologically-oriented behaviourism as foundation. Because the researchers had no relation to the language they studied, all introspection was excluded. They were forced to base their researches on objective, mostly phonological and symbolic attributes that could be perceived directly. The usual ways of procedure, based on intuition, thenceforth appeared as a mystification. A new ideal of being scientific entered the linguistic field. The new methodology was applied to the linguistic subject, and a description resulted which was able to state its object more precisely in terminologies that were independent of language.

This synopsis necessarily leads to the conclusion that Parisian structuralism, which has become fashionable today, is no more than a recapitulation of what has been presented here — only in this sense can we speak of it as being a further development of structuralist thinking. The same themes and methods are being discussed anew. What is being presented to us as *dernier cri* is at best a differentiation, or an expansion, of these themes, or else a revision of them undertaken under the influence of new scientific insights.

CHAPTER IV

PARIS

1. CONSTELLATIONS

'The same, but different' — this would be a good motto for the activities of
the Parisian structuralists. The phrase gives us a lead in many respects. Today's
structuralism, mainly French, is like structuralist thinking before World War
II, but with changed perspectives and in new arrangements. The several
circles that nowadays go to make up Parisian structuralism study the same
themes as did previous structuralists, although they approach them differently.

This holds also for the many themes which structuralists share with other
philosophical trends, such as existentialism. Today's structuralism studies
the same fundamental problems, but follows different principles. That becomes clear once we compare Sartre's and Althusser's studies of Marxism.
They differ substantially from one another in their respective philosophical
stands, but they share the same perspectives nevertheless. They are not for
instance interested in problems of a planned economy, in economic policy,
or in market mechanisms, as studied by Marx and described in *Das Kapital*
or in *Grundrissen der Kritik der politischen Oekonomie.*

The same may be said about literature as a theme. It is certainly represented in all Parisian structuralism, but, though there may be similarity with
Czech structuralism, a considerable differentiation nevertheless has arisen.
Sociology, linguistics, psychoanalysis, semiotics (that is closely related to
formal logic), as well as a new understanding of hermeneutical question
produced the material out of which a structural view of literature was
built up. The philosophical component is always present, but seldom
manifests itself in an autonomous rôle. Nevertheless, a continuous link
with philosophical tradition is virtually a *sine qua non* for French structuralists. Classic figures in philosophy like Plato, Hegel, Rousseau, and
Nietzsche, together with present-day philosophers such as Husserl and
Heidegger are represented — more so than they are represented in the work
of the Prague Circle. We also find here that the structuralists share interest
in Marx, Nietzsche, Plato, or Hegel with the existentialists, but one might say
that structuralism reads the same texts differently. Not until structuralism
do they indeed actually become *texts.*

Finally, our motto, strictly interpreted, represents a philosophical theme which was revived again by the structuralists — the theme of *identity and difference*. The autonomy of the formalist approach sought to uphold what is *identical* in all the differentiations brought about by science and phenomenality. These differentiations are to be found in all cultural-anthropological, linguistic, and philosophical approaches without the concept of *identity*, however, disappearing — the identity is indeed even corroborated by differentiality. This indicates the particular stress laid by structuralism on the highly relevant problem of order.

The fact, already mentioned, that there were several circles within Parisian structuralism, reminds us of the *kružki* in Russian formalism or of the later linguistic Circles. Today's 'circles', however, are more like distinguishably different *milieux*, expressing the fashion of the day. They are unstructured groups, with certain people, texts, or themes as foci, often directly and invariably indirectly linked with an educational institution. We do not in the first place have the Sorbonne in mind (where especially the *Faculté des Lettres et Sciences Humaines* is still mainly preoccupied with the history of philosophy), nor Nanterre where philosophers like Dufrenne (an opponent of structuralism), Ricoeur, and Levinas are at work. These philosophers are interested in the classics of philosophy, but also in Marx, Kierkegaard, Nietzsche, Heidegger, and Husserl. Ricoeur discusses structuralism in his hermeneutics, and studies present-day analytical philosophy of language, particularly of Anglo-Saxon origin. The *Collège de France* is much closer to structuralism, where open lectures are given, without the need to enrol for training or diplomas. The interlocking of philosophy, linguistics, and cultural anthropology (so specific a characteristic of structuralist thinking), comes out clearly here. The fact that Lévi-Strauss (ethnology), Benveniste (linguistics), and recently Foucault (philosophy) and Aron (sociology) all lecture at the *Collège* illustrates the point.

Another centre of structuralist activity is the *École des Hautes Études*, a semi-academic institution that organises lectures and seminars. The important linguists Martinet and Greimas work there, as does Roland Barthes who has become famous as semiologist and critic. The well-known *École Normale Supérieure* also owes much to structuralist thinking — in its *Cercle d'épistémologie* Jacques Derrida and Louis Althusser (the specialist on Marx who is connected with the publishing group Maspéro) are to be found.

Finally, there are independent centres, not related to educational institutions. Jacques Lacan, for instance, is connected with a therapeutic institution, the clinic *Sainte-Anne*. The group *Tel Quel* is associated with the journal of that name. Although the boundaries of such circles may be somewhat diffuse, a certain basic approach remains clearly recognizable. This holds primarily for linguistics, without which for instance neither Lacan's psychoanalysis nor Roland Barthes's literary criticism is conceivable. The rôle modern linguistics plays is more or less that of a kind of mathematics for structuralist epistemological work in art, literature, philosophy, psychology, and the social sciences. In this regard, the linguistics emanating from Geneva (de Saussure), the Prague Circle (Trubetzkoy, Jakobson), and the Copenhagen circle (Hjelmslev) remain important, as does the further elaboration of Chomsky's idea of a 'generative grammar'. Moreover, the linguistic contributions of Martinet, Benveniste, and Greimas play a large part in French structuralism. Their influence in various fields is clearly visible — in the structural anthropology of Lévi-Strauss, in Julia Kristeva's semiology, in similar works of Jean Starobinsky, and in Jacques Lacan's psychoanalysis. The same goes for the literary criticism of Roland Barthes, Lucien Goldmann, and other contributors to the group *Tel Quel.*

In French structuralism, as in Russian formalism, literary aesthetics seem the most obvious point of departure for structuralist theory. This is illustrated by the publications of the *Tel Quel* group, such as their journal, founded in 1960, and the book *Théorie d'ensemble*, which appeared in 1968. It also applies to revived attempts at a literary and general hermeneutics — this revival received its impulse from structuralism. Not only the *Tel Quel* group but also representatives of a so-called 'genetic structuralism', such as the philosopher Derrida and the sociologist Goldmann, have contributed to the revival of literary hermeneutics. We should also mention literary criticism which, following upon Sartre, Mauron, and Poulet (*4.19*), was carried further in a structuralist direction by Goldmann, Starobinsky, and especially by Roland Barthes.

2. PARISIAN STRUCTURALISM

A. *Tel Quel and Formalism*

Tel Quel is a group, a journal, and a series of publications. Philippe Sollers (founder of the journal) and Jean Ricardou are two of the chief participants in this wide-ranging activity. The work of writers like Kristeva, Pleynet, Derrida, Thibeaudau, and others should be included. Connexions with Russian formalism were consciously sought and cultivated, as was the closely related interest in linguistics, especially in the Geneva School. Their analyses are concerned with material, which to them would not be amenable to a biographical, sociological, or psychological approach, nor indeed to an approach via the history of literature. For language is much more than only the bearer of meanings and does not need any extraliterary justification. The resemblance to Russian formalism, especially in its initial form, is thus apparent. These French writers also concern themselves with analyses, which respect, or even advance, the idea of the autonomy of language. For this, linguistics is *par excellence* the means; with its help we may master, not only the analysis, but also the hermeneutic problem.

In the first place, the conventional concept of *meaning*, in contrast to the principle of *interpretation,* now acquires a functional sense. Todorov, publisher of the first French collection of Russian formalist texts, argues that the meaning of a literary element consists in the possibilities for function which we give that element. A word, a metaphor, a dialogue therefore has that meaning which it acquires through mutual relations with other elements in that particular text. The interpretation thus depends on the personality of the reader, who picks the element out of the whole context, and fits it into a new system (such as an economic, ideological, historical, or biological system) thus assessing it according to his own standards. If this functional conception limits the number of possible meanings of a text-element (this limitation depending on what kind of text it is), the number of possible interpretations remains in principle, however, unlimited. This functionalist view, focussed on the language as material and on literature as *opus*, takes the traditional problem of interpretation, and the inherent problem of the relation between author and reader (illustrated by Sartre's idealistic contribution dated 1948, *Qu'est-ce-que la littérature?*), a considerable step further. A theory of writing now becomes possible – a theory of the relationship between the author on the one hand and the language and the reader on the other. This theory preserves the autonomy of language and *opus;* writing does not impart already-existing knowledge, but explores what is possible in the language and extends the independence of the language. The literary text therefore does not, in a servile way, pass on a meaning the author had in mind, but it creates a structure, presented to the reader as a set of forms that expect to be imbued with sense (Genette). This principle once more suggests formalism – it is not the content, which stipulates a certain form, but the form which constantly creates its content. Thus, as with Russian formalism, *Tel Quel* theories imply alienation. Only by alienation can we arrive at a limited plurality of meaning and an unlimited plurality of interpretation. The idea of a compelling language, an everyday language that is unequivocal and all too easily understood, had to be done away with, so that new possibilities for language and a new understanding of it could be opened up. The productivity which is characteristic of language requires a causality, not the authority of the author's subjective way of expression. Instead of literature (as a form of subjective authority) we think of the production of texts (Sollers).

Following such lines of thought, the producing, writing subject is therefore decentralized, and this comes across as an act of liberation. Freedom which enables the depth structure of a text to function is achieved because we are liberated in several ways : we have insight into the writer's commitments, we have insight into the ideological nature of all literature that sets out to no more than convey meanings, and the subjective authority of the author is no longer imposed upon us. Every text creates new patterns of relationships, and makes things possible which even the author does not understand. Hence the difficulty in beginning and in developing these texts. The essential forfeit of the author's self in the deeper structure of the text becomes apparent. Sollers describes this very clearly in his novel *Drame*:

> No beginning ever gives the essential guarantee of neutrality ... Surprise: he had always believed that he could tell the real story at the very moment he wanted to do so ... . If he were really to try to do that, every day, during the brief moments when he and his plan are identical – right down to the horror, to the nothingness – he would have to start at random, masking the risk by his cunning ... . He would soon have the impression that he had by mistake strayed into an animated museum, in which he himself was simultaneously the peripheral and the central figure in all the paintings: none of them would have the same form or the same author. He would have to carry on from there. (*4.20*, 11, 12)

Moreover, the so-called 'alien' texts are not citations, or irrelevant fragments like foreign bodies. In a different context, such fragments open up new phonetic and conceptual possibilities, and constantly introduce new combinations, so that the copyright question of with whom they originated becomes senseless. Julia Kristeva therefore distinguishes *phéno-texte* (the expressed communication) from *géno-texte* (meanings generating other meanings). The latter are the most important; *géno-textes* are of central interest to the *Tel Quel* group. All texts originate in the subjective and seek the collective, where the autarchy of the text presumably is better assured. No text ever originates solely from the creative consciousness of a writer – it originates from other texts and is written from the vantage that they provide. Kristeva therefore speaks of *intertextualité* (*4.17*; 284), which concerns the text *in* the text (Starobinsky), the continuous relevance of all texts, overlapping and combinations, as well as functional relationships and their ever-changing structures.

B. *Hermeneutics and Genetic Structuralism*

From all of these sources, the new hermeneutics, particularly literary hermeneutics, draws inspiration. Its new insights also go back to structural functionalism, a functionalism which results from the priority de Saussure accorded the synchronical. Lucien Goldmann, in his *Marxisme et sciences humaines* (1970), tries to produce a genetic structuralism in which the diachronical and the synchronical are reconciled. Such reconciliation meliorates the overly dogmatic-formalistic consequences of the *Tel Quel* theories, especially where the rôle of the subject is concerned. The history of the development of Russian formalism showed that only a synthesis of the diachronical and the synchronical could be fruitful. This idea leads also to a better understanding of Czech structuralism. The same applies to the formalist thinking of the *Tel-Quel* group and to other genetic and hermeneutical theories, for these (and especially the latter) are inspired by the thought of such a synthesis. This is true of Goldmann's work as well as of Paul Ricoeur's hermeneutics: *Le conflit des interprétations* (1969). Apart from studies of symbols, and studies in belief and religion, Ricoeur's book contains contributions towards defining the position of today's hermeneutics in relation to structuralism, phenomenology, and psychoanalysis. Ricoeur argues that analysis of symbols and interpretation support hermeneutical activity, because they help to overcome the limitations of semantics. A symbol is any structure of meaning in which a direct, primary, literal sense is set alongside another, indirect, secondary, figurative sense, so that the latter can only be understood through the former. The interpretation, to which Ricoeur also devoted a study (*4.6*), is related to the symbol and to hermeneutics. Interpretation is any activity which decodes the latent sense and makes it manifest, discovering what is hidden at all the levels of meaning that the literal meaning implies. This two-fold way of overcoming the limitations of semantics by analysing the symbol and by interpretation gives rise to a multiplicity of problems, which, taken one by one, certainly do not lead to a unification of problems in hermeneutics. On the contrary, as is understandable, every interpretation reduces the wealth of symbolism in terms of the specific pattern of the literature in question. The form of the interpretation corresponds to the theoretical structure of the hermeneutical system concerned. Analysing the semantic structure of such expressions as have a multiple sense may perhaps open the door to a unifying philosophical view, but the semantic problems in themselves are not the same as philosophical problems. If we wish to develop a truly philosophical hermeneutics that will bring about uniform interpretation, then we shall have to be able to relate language to the very process of being. The process of becoming human after all rests fundamentally upon language. This becomes clear in psychoanalysis, when awareness is brought about through discussion. There are, however, more obscure languages: in the myth, in the metaphor, in the dream. The Cartesian principle *cogito ergo sum* is not the point of departure but the result of this process. Knowledge in this case means self-realization. Knowledge of the world and knowledge of oneself have a close dialectical relationship. That is the existential foundation of the hermeneutical circle, and the basis for a truly genetic structuralism.

Life as a text; self-realization as an on-going interpretation of the continuously differentiated text, composed of eros and poetry, of idealism and belief, of suffering, desire, good and evil. For Ricoeur, however, hermeneutics is not just reading. It does not only have to do with a horizontal effort on my part, because the hierarchical order system of others impinges upon me, and introduces the vertical. The lower must be understood *via* the higher. Such thoughts bring Ricoeur close to Levinas and to philosophers of dialogue like Rosenzweig, Löwith, Ebner, and Buber. But there are links even with Marx. Lucien Goldmann refers to Marx and his reversal of the current theory of evolution: human anatomy is a key to the anatomy of the ape. Nicolai Hartmann should be mentioned here, and particularly Max Scheler. Both changed their emphasis in considering the horizontal and the vertical, or 'what' causes the 'higher' and the 'lower'. Such reversal is appropriate to hermeneutics; listening to the spoken word enables us to speak. Semantic implication, too, depends on listening. For, as Ricoeur argues, the subjectivity of speech is at the same time the inter-subjectivity of address. This goes for the spoken word *(parole parlée)* as well as for the actual address *(parole parlante)*.

The hermeneutical problem proceeds from here. Instead of 'Truth and Method' (Gadamer, *4.3*) its theme becomes 'Language and Method'. And once again the central point is (as Ricoeur makes clear in his criticism) that de Saussure sought to separate the inseparable. Language as *langue* (as a system) cannot be separated from language as *parole* (as speech, as what happens). Translated into structuralist terminology, this means that the diachronical and the synchronical belong together. The unity of system and unique event has to be re-established despite the formalist attempts at separation which, starting with the Geneva linguists, dominated the earlier Russian formalists and (to a considerable extent) also the *Tel Quel* theorists. This is Ricoeur's purpose and his basis for discussion. Concretely, it implies the re-establishment of the unity between language and speech, which is seen as a dialectic product of the system as system and the system as an act. Structure appears as a unique happening. The conclusion from all of this would be that history and subjectivity regain their former status. The question: 'Who speaks?' re-acquires the sense it lost on the level of *langue*. Only here does a new chance appear to link up hermeneutics and linguistics. This would contribute to the understanding of human self-realization, a realization characterized at the same time by horizontal intentionality and by vertical relevation of the other.

Speech occurs when a subject in an act, in a single moment of speech, takes up the system of signs which language keeps in store for him. The system remains virtual as long as it is not fulfilled, realized, or employed by somebody who at the same time turns to somebody else. The subjectivity of the act of speech is at the same time the inter-subjectivity of an address. *(4.7) (0.12,* 218)

C. *Literary Criticism and Semiology*

The problems of literary criticism should be mentioned in this regard, especially in connexion with the semiology of Roland Barthes and Julia Kristeva. The debate between the older French criticisms and the more modern ones is comprehensively covered in Serge Doubrovsky's book: *Pourquoi la novuelle critique?* (1966). The issue is a certain relationship between two *milieux* of literary criticism. On the one hand there is the academic, traditional criticism, whose object is to elucidate literary work by means of extra-literary analogies, and on the other hand there is the new criticism which, via Sartre's existential criticism, Mauron's psychoanalytical criticism, Starobinsky's thematic criticism, Goldmann's sociological criticism, and Barthes's formalist criticism, has become in a sense a (widely ramified) tradition of our own time. Two important insights are characteristic of Barthes's opinions. They link his theses concerning the authenticity of the literary with the hermeneutical problems mentioned. The first insight concerns the relation between literature and language, and it raises the same problem of identity and difference as is to be found in de Saussure's relation between *langue* and *parole*. Secondly, Barthes argues (in much the same tradition as Sartre in his essay of 1948) that writing essentially has the characteristics of dialogue. He refers to the specificity of the process of writing, which links literary form and conceptuality with one another. Moreover, only this process can save the meaning of a text from becoming paralysed, and hence merely an *ensemble* of dead words. Here again we see a genetic, dynamic structuralism at work.

Barthes's first insight is based upon a change in the meaning of what language is and upon a shift in the relationship between the work itself and the external factors that determine it. In the course of the eighteenth century, says Barthes, and particularly towards the end of the nineteenth century — Flaubert (*4.62*), Mallarmé — language was appreciated as an art, and literature as a form. The subsequent development of Russian formalism, which also falls back on Flaubert and Mallarmé, supports this insight. Writing becomes a

function. In structural thought bearing the Czech stamp, and also in the early
sociology of literature, a functional link between the creative and the social
becomes a major object. Trotzky had already taken a stand against this
change in his exchanges with the Moscow Circle. Writing becomes a feature
of a literary, fashion-bound language, which has a social rôle to fulfil, and
literature is thus reduced to its nadir. *(4.8)* The shift in the relation between
the work and its position vis-à-vis the environment presents a parallel case.
The idea of the work as a creative product, with its own sources, history of
origin, influence and effect, is supplanted by the idea of the literary work as
a sign for something lying beyond the work. Consequently it always has to be
decoded.

The hermetically sealed position of the work is thus opened up and new
hermeneutical and critical possibilities arise. The literary, if it is seen as language material, has a meaning which does not coincide with the meaning of
that which makes literature literature (Jakobson, in the beginning of the
twenties, spoke of *literaturnost*). Consequently, within the concrete unity
of literary signs, there are at least two constituent systems of signs. The first
is that of the communication of language – linguistics distinguishes *signifié*
(concept), *signification* (meaning) and *signifiant* (indicator; that which makes
the sign manifest). The second is a system which subsumes the first system
within itself. Within this second system, the first system functions as an
indicator. The study of the identity and the difference of these two systems
is the task of semiology and of criticism (in Barthes's sense). Literature
therefore contains within itself a system of signs which is basically strange to
it. Hence literature becomes a parasite on language. The same goes for myth
and for fashion.

The following consequences of this new criticism, in the context of
modern hermeneutics, are important for structuralist thinking.

(i) The text an author produces achieves more than what he strove for;
his activity is intransitive; his text has multiple meanings. The assembly of
indicators, as put together by the author, does not in any way control the
existence of the *signifiés*, the meanings. The secondary system of literature
always renders the informative content of his text relative.

(ii) Although the openness of the text may indeed be seen as a semantic
openness, it manifests itself more clearly as an openness focussed on dialogue. Literature is a questioning. The author is not in a position to give final
answers; at best he gives partial answers, which in their turn evoke new
questions, and create new forms and meanings for others. All indicators re-
quire the chance to fulfil their meaning. Literature exists by means of this
process of fulfilment, a process which aims at the self-realization of the

literary. For this reason, Barthes, in his work *Racine*, speaks of the essential dialogue between reader and author, of contra-communication, and of literature as "intentional cartography".

(iii) Such thinking renders the problem of meaning essentially dynamic. Meaning is not a static concept. It is the process which leads from form *(forme)* to concept *(concept)*, i.e. to the *signifié*. Thus literature is determined by the way in which the form achieves conceptuality. The connotation provides a secondary meaning, which meaning follows from a new system of signs. This different system in turn is integrated into that system as *signifiant*. The general dynamic character of this concept of 'meaning' enables us to study the systems character of that process. To do this, we should subject text, fashion, mythology, and other similar themes to semiological analysis. When we interpret the concept of meaning more dynamically, when we 'open up' the literary text, when we decentralize the authority-producing literary subject, we not only discover the formalistic component but we also make a fresh attempt to synthesize the synchronic and the diachronic, despite all the differences in these two linguistic aspects *as language*. Dogmatic formalism thus gives way to the semiological approach, which is essentially a synthesizing approach.

The place which functionalist, formalist, and structuralist criticisms occupy in general literary criticism deviates markedly from traditional criticism which concentrates exclusively on the creative mind. This latter is brilliantly represented by Sartre and particularly by Georges Poulet (*4.19*). According to Poulet, it is the reader's aim to come upon a first experience which is empathetic and which can be presented dialectically. Criticism starts from this experience, and takes place in the field of tension that arises between, on the one hand, the autarchial consciousness of the author, and, on the other hand, the reader's and critic's adaption. The former makes the the more important contribution, because the latter two have to adapt to the author's tempo. This means that they have to get close to him, and to spot the secret of his life, his feelings, and his thinking. To grasp a literary work therefore involves reading, recognizing, and understanding from the position of a central consciousness. Such understanding represents the ideal act of criticism. Often only fragments of the work are present with the reader and only by comprehensive retrospection can the work be seen in its totality. The complete work of a poet is of a monadic character; it represents a universalistic totality. Understanding this totality is a prerequisite for all criticism — it depends exclusively on the inter-subjective experience on the author meeting his reader and the reader his author. The more objective features of the literary work, such as structure, form, genre, etc.,

play a subsidiary part in these observations, which differ entirely from structuralist thought. On this account, the critic Jean Rousset has reservations,
but his reservations do not go so far as to lead him to espouse the more radical point of view. He tries instead to reconcile objective and subjective approaches. Poetry should in the first place be experienced as form, as language. The observant reader, however, should, in the second round as it
were, gradually link the formal features with the content so that the characteristic and unique structure of the work may in due course be realized.

Whether literary criticism to a greater or lesser extent coincides with
linguistics is an important question – a question which the group *Tel Quel*
does not answer definitively. The above-mentioned formalist and semiological studies, with their functionalist implications, could easily give the
impression that there indeed was such coincidence. Rousset as well as
Doubrovsky would, however, decidedly disagree. The philosophical problems of literary criticism come to life when linguistics and criticism go different ways. Several authors of the *Tel Quel* group might have had such
experience at first hand, as they not only acted as critics but also as creative
writers. The human sciences may make many contributions to literary criticism, but only criticism as such is in a position to grasp the unity and totality of
all the meanings constituting the sense of a work. The great ideologies represented in modern literature, such as structuralism, psychoanalysis, and
Marxism, all create their own fields of meaning and their own units of interpretation, but they do not manage to create from those a unity from which
the literary work may be integrally understood. This claim, previously made
by philosophical aesthetes, now comes from structuralist criticism. Problems
concerning a unified understanding of a work of art are, however, problems
which are predominantly epistemological. What philosophy of the present
day can bring about such unity?

D. *Psychoanalysis and Linguistics*

Jacques Lacan's psychoanalysis *(4.28)*, closely related to structural linguistics, ranks among the most important contributions of present-day French
structuralism. His main goal, both in his Paris clinic *Saint-Anne* and in the
École Normale Supérieure, is to develop psychoanalysis into an independent
and self-contained scientific theory. Only with the aid of structural linguistics can the subconscious be described in scientific terms, and can its laws be
understood. By means of this insight, Lacan arrives at a number of basic
statements, all referring to the structure of the human discourse *(discours)*.
Thus psychoanalytical theories are brought within the sphere of the modern
human sciences. The best-known and most fundamental statements are prob-

ably: "The discourse of the unconscious is structured as a language", and "The unconscious is the discourse of the other". One has to bear in mind that 'the other' for Lacan does not only mean the other person, but also the order of the language (seen as it were through the subject's eyes) which creates both the trans-individual culture and the subconscious in the subject. We have here two important aspects of the psychoanalytical approach to the process of human development: the language of the unconscious is *recognized as a language,* and *the presence of the other in this language structure is recognized.*

Lacan's objective is to make a contemporarily relevant theory out of traditional psychoanalysis. Equally, however, does he wish to associate himself with today's structuralist fashion. He thus influences various literary and philosophical ideas such as those of Blanchot, Foucault, Ortigues, Barthes and Althusser. It should be stressed that Lacan does not wish to develop a *new* psychoanalytical theory, but is attempting to raise Freud's theory to a scientific level. His principal writings, collated in one volume, *Écrits,* have therefore been issued in a series explicitly called *Le champ freudien.* It is also noteworthy that Lacan's writings do not only contain a psychoanalytical theory but equally important views on society, views that often bring him close to the Marxist Althusser. Lacan's essay on aggression in psychoanalysis, *L'agressivité en psychoanalyse,* contains a theory about today's ideology of freedom as it appears in the concept of free enterprise or in the principle of competition in industry, study, or sport. This ideology is exposed as being an alibi for other ideologies, and in this a parallel is seen with the appeal of Althusser and Foucault for an anti-humanism, because humanism, too, has become an alibi for other, often inhuman, goals and views.

It also becomes clear, for instance in *La science et la vérité,* that Lacan's effort to incorporate linguistics into psychoanalysis has consequences which closely resemble the similar effort of Althusser to incorporate linguistic analysis into Marxism. Althusser himself has indicated how psychoanalysts, by using the approach of structural linguistics, find themselves in a position where they can both accept Freud's theories and take conscious account of the social and economic conditions for such acceptance. True enough, this primarily holds for analytical practice, but on a different level it is also of great import for the theory itself. The invariable presence of the other reveals the social and economic conditions for human development.

This also puts an end to the wearisome and complicated efforts to turn psychoanalysis into an ideology. Hitherto we have seen many different attempts to incorporate psychoanalysis into some more comprehensive theory. Examples are Sartre's existentialism, Merleau-Ponty's phenomenology,

Dalbiez's behaviourism, the sociology and cultural anthropology of Kardiner, Mead *et al.*, and of Ludwig Binswanger's *Daseins*-analysis. Such integration has usually been based on the fallacy that psychoanalysis does not present an independent theory, but basically is nothing more than a practice, without a clear objective that can be justified on grounds of theory. A structuralist reading of Freud should make it possible to determine the objective of psychoanalysis scientifically, and so put an end to the situation mentioned above.

The structure of the personality is an articulation on several levels of language, these levels themselves being structured. For psychoanalysis this means that it is not the dream which counts as the most important psychoanalytical document, but the conversation *(discours)* about it, which differs from the dream. This document is linked to the structure of language on different levels. Every patient presents to the analyst both a document and an interpretation of it, which itself is yet another document. The analyst consequently has to take up a complementary attitude, characterized by Freud as *Konstruktion.*

... The patient ought to be led to remember something of what he has experienced, and of what he has repressed. The dynamic relations in such process are so interesting that the other part of the work, what the analyst does, fades into the background. The analyst has neither experienced nor repressed anything that is relevant; it cannot be his task to recall something. What, then, is his task? He has to guess what was forgotten from the signs it left behind, or, better still, he has *to construct* it. How, why, and with what explication he imparts his constructions to the patient produces the relation between the two parts of the analytical work; his own contribution, and that of the patient. (*4.27, 45*)

The constructive nature of the relation between analyst and patient is linguistic in character. The construction achieved in the relationship necessarily belongs to the structural field, either *via* conversation or a text (*4.24; 61 ff.*)

The need for construction stems from the fact that the patient's own uncovering of his psychical structure must always be fragmentary and incoherent. For every human being basically develops from conflict situations; he cannot evade being frustrated, and the fulfilment of his desires is always dependent either on Nature or on other human beings. Lacan quotes Hegel in this regard: Human desire is only satisfied through the desire and work of the other. Lacan also often quotes a fragment from the *Phänomenology des Geistes*, where Hegel speaks of the relationship between master and servant. In the dynamic master-servant relationship, it is the servant who has the possibility of *becoming* something (but also of losing his existence!), whereas the master already *is* something, and the disadvantageous aspects of the advantage of being master soon become clear to him.

What this is about and why it is important in Lacan's reading of Freud cannot be understood without a careful study of the closely related problem of recognition (*Anerkennung*). The transposition of desire into *question*, a transposition achieved by Freud and particularly by Lacan, is based on the possibility of recognition. With such transposition, the *question* appears to be the symbolic place where alienation becomes independent of the original desire. The *recognized* consciousness and the *recognising* consciousness rediscover one another as parts of the same total structure. This is the deeper meaning of what Hegel says, but presumably also that of Freud's concept of construction. In either case one comes up against the multi-purpose and many-sided structure of recognition, because all moments to which language brings independence can only be recognized as such if their mutual relativity is understood. Hegel's words then become relevant: self-consciousness can only mean *recognised* self-consciousness; it does not end in the other, or confronting the other, but it finds itself in the other by means of recognition. (*4.25*, 30) (*0.9*, 142 ff.)

From all of the foregoing it follows that an absolute subconscious, as a kind of repository for temporarily unused memories, or as a *deus ex machina*, which has to solve all problems of consciousness, no longer exists. As 'speech of the other' it is conversation: relative or marginal. It is speech because it belongs to the *discours*, to the order in language and culture. It is relative because what is conscious for one is (still) subconscious for the other. It is marginal because it does not indicate any limits to what our consciousness does — limits which are experienced in the order of language, particularly in discussion between oneself and the other. And so a totally different model of the subconscious emerges, a relative and marginal one — a different model of psychic life in general. It no longer is a continuous battle between more-or-less independent psychical forces and tendencies (what a strange social picture determines this interpretation of the psyche, focussing as it does upon competition) nor does it consist of constantly cancelling out diachronical moments of life. Lacan seeks, by means of the difference that is shown up here, to bring about a final separation between psychoanalysis and psychology.

Not the dream, but language, especially as it is used in speech, is the most important 'document' in psychoanalysis. Two processes are stressed in Freud's *Traumdeutung* ('Interpretation of Dreams'), 1900. These processes he identifies as *Verdichtingsarbeit* and *Verschiebungsarbeit*, which may be freely translated as making the meaning more condensed — and thus more manageable — and displacing the meaning elsewhere. We see here the essential difference, mentioned above, between dreams and discourse. "The dream

is scant, sparse, laconic, when compared with the scope and wealth of content in the thoughts behind the dream. The dream, written down, takes up
half a page ..." Continuing: "The elements which, according to the content
of the dream, appear essential, do not play nearly the same rôle in the
thoughts behind the dream. What is obviously the real content of the
thoughts behind the dream we do not necessarily find in the dream at all."
(4.26, 284, 310) Lacan recognises in *Verdichtungsarbeit* the figure of speech
called *metonymy* (displacement of meaning) and in *Verschiebungsarbeit* the
figure of speech we know as *metaphor.* (4.28, 511) The road to structuralist
interpretation now lies open. Lacan builds formalizations upon these figures
of speech. With metonymy he assimilates concepts such as combination, displacement, and diachrony; with metaphor concepts such as substitution, condensation, and synchrony. In Lacan's view, Freud undertook his interpretation of dreams along the two important axes of language: combination - displacement = metaphor, and substitution - condensation = metonymy.

The primacy thus ascribed to the formal structure of language and its
immanent mechanisms renders superfluous a number of (mainly idealistic)
philosophical interpretations of the subconscious and its relation to the conscious. We think of Sartre's idea of the *mauvaise foi*, of Merleau-Ponty's
idea of the unconscious as a residuum of the conscious, of biological and
archetypical interpretations like those of Jung. Althusser calls such interpretations "ideological errors of thought". The linguistic approach shows that
the facts at issue are empirical, not only symbolic.

When the 'self' speaks, its speech is also the discourse of the other.
This goes for everyday speech, and equally for the subconscious. Lacan
refers to two important aspects of the psychoanalytical interpretation of the
history of human growth: first and foremost to the oedipal situation,
and to the experience of reflexion (*stade du miroir*). Both the dual, pre-
oedipal situation and the dualistic oedipal situation are dominated by the
laws of symbolic order. Where its formal structure is concerned, the symbolic might, superficially, be confused with the order of language. In the oedipal phase, the language order (which is at the same time the order of the
culture) after all plays a part, both in conversation and as a medium that
determines and creates meanings. To enter this order is to enter a *discours*
which then becomes a presupposition for all speech: the discourse of
the order itself, the discourse of the other, the discourse of a third (which
is order) i.e. the subconscious. The entry into the order of speech does
not only take place when the biological being first encounters sexual
differentiation (and thus, according to Lacan, gains access to the symbolical-
linguistic order) but each time when, in the field of tension of the analyst-

therapist situation, the subject reveals the truth by what he says. This holds good for Lacan as it held good for Freud: the truth of analysis is in the inter-subjective and analytical *discours*. This truth is not stated once and for all. It lives because it is repeated — it is re-achieved anew in every stage of human development.

With observations such as these, Lacan tries to get a conceptual grip on the subconscious. It is the place where every individual is situated within his own language — wherever that language may be sought, missed, or forced into; wherever it would like to break out, and wherever it has to stay precise-ly so that it may be able to break out. In this linguistically-conceived oedi-pal influence, the structural approach resolves the 'conflict' between oedipal freedom and determination. The biological being, afflicted with sexuality, becomes a sexualised human being, becomes a man or a woman, a father or a mother. This determination, when a successful determination, (Szilase), is at the same time a liberation. To state this in a more formalized way: Phallus, father, the good, the law. There are formal schemes of order which do not have to be evoked, by means of ritual practice, as symbols or deeply hidden struc-tures, but are instead "dramatic structures" (Lacan) which, being part of the order of culture, are inseparable from the process of human development. He who develops within a culture only has to listen. In this we find an apparent similarity with the thoughts of Ricoeur, a similarity which should not, how-ever, mislead us. Lacan calls Ricoeur a "metaphysical ventriloquist," because Ricoeur sees psychoanalysis as a symbolical series, to be interpreted as a sign that does not relate to any human discourse, but to the Word as spoken by God. Lacan finds this verticality superfluous, because the order is already to be found in the horizontality of the language up to the oedipal stage. Listen-ing to that order is to be a human. The contrast between the synchronical and the diachronical, between structure and history, thus basically disappears in the oedipal phase, the disappearance being brought about by repetition. This repetition is in itself communication, because the sender gets his own message in transposed form back from the recipient. Only a non-response brings the process to a standstill, and makes of it a paralysed structure. This at the same time implies the destruction of the subject.

These thoughts suggest that dialogue has influenced structuralism. Frater-nity and love are concepts Lacan often employs. In close correspondence with Martin Buber, Lacan holds that the realization of love is not a fruit of Nature, but *grace*, i.e. an inter-subjective agreement which can only be fully realized when the subject is decentralized. Isn't this a "ventriloquism" similar to that of which Ricoeur was accused? Does Lacan not see that love as grace implies verticality? Besides, what is left here of a formalist, functionalist structuralism when it seems that the *parole parlante* nevertheless has precedence over the *parole parlée*? Because for Lacan structure is not an ideational model that can be distinguished from reality by its intelligibility, and therefore may be true or false, adequate or inadequate (as it is for Lévi-Strauss). In psychoanalytic terminology the structure of the truth of the *discours* is such that it can only be formulated in the *discours* itself. Structuralism therefore is the field of this discourse, where the truth shapes itself.

Since 1958, Lacan has dissociated himself more and more from the way in which Freud sought to constitute the object of psychoanalysis. Concomitantly, and particularly as renewed attempt to get closer to this object, formalism has been resorted to. The theoretical foundations for this are already to be found in the well-known working paper from his 1955 seminar: *La lettre volée*. It illustrates how the object disappears within the complex network of contextualities, contextualities which, because of the structural character implicit in them, can be formalized. At the same time, it shows us how Lacan resists any interpretation, on the basis of either dialogue or ontology, of the processes he attacks. It also implies dissociation from Hegel and from surrealism, i.e. from important stadia in Lacan's own philosophical development. On the other hand, it demonstrates a tendency, stemming from Jakobson's linguistics, to objectify and to formalize.

E. *Structural Anthropology and Epistemology*

The very substantial, varied, and wide-ranging *Échanges et communications* (*4.30*), published in 1970 in honour of Lévi-Strauss's sixtieth birthday, illustrates how much fruit the work of this ethnologist has borne, not only in his own professional field, but in many other fields of scientific and literary thinking. It is hardly possible, nor would it serve our purpose, to try to survey his contributions here. The central question is to what extent Lévi-Strauss's approaches and researches in cultural anthropology have contributed not only to present-day structuralism but more generally to epistemological questions of our time. Epistemology is primarily to be understood as a generic problem in cultural philosophy, secondly as a philosophical problem in a stricter sense of the term. Lévi-Strauss himself confirms this more than once and it is the main point made in the above-mentioned commemorative volume. The sociologist and philosopher Raymond Aron, whose contribution to this volume deals with the paradox of the self and the other, (*Le paradoxe du même et de l'autre, 4.30,* 943ff.) also deals with the extent to which Lévi-Strauss's structural analysis in cultural anthropology is relevant for epistemology and for the theory of science. Is the structural analysis of Lévi-Strauss really analytical, or is it much more subjective, depending upon the sudden impulses of an individual scholar. Doesn't the clarity with which we understand how the human spirit expresses itself in the various mythologies in accordance with a basic uniformity depend solely upon the intelligibility of the relevant researcher? (Lévi-Strauss,*Mythologies*, Vol.I: *Le cru et le cuit;* Vol. II: *Du miel aux cendres*; Vol. III: *L'origine des manières de table,* Vol. IV: *L'homme nu, 4.37*).

As already mentioned in the first chapter, Lévi-Strauss sought to ensure the scientific nature of his observations by his use of the linguistic and particularly the phonological method. The wish to be scientific in his procedure Lévi-Strauss shares with Lacan, with many structuralist thinkers, with representatives of the group *Tel Quel*, and with formalists of more than one generation. For linguistics has but one universal object: the articulated language. Moreover, the methodology of linguistics is almost homogeneous, based on principles on which all specialists agree. Neither such arguments themselves, however, nor the linking of such arguments to the explication of the concept of structure, brings us any step closer to the realm of philosophy. Lévi-Strauss has never misled his readers where philosophy is concerned. Although he presents them with views and perspectives of a general cultural-philosophic kind — which are very interesting, and are reminiscent, as we have said, of Nietzsche and often also of Rousseau and Marx (*4.42*, 113ff.) — it has never been his intention to draw strictly philosophical conclusions from cultural anthropology. Quite the contrary: he emphasizes that he never hesitates to make his own use of even the most different and often contradictory philosophical points of view, if by doing so he might contribute to the understanding of a style of life, an institution, a belief. Philosophical arguments, to him, are but improvised pedestals on which to place his precious objects in order to demonstrate their value. It is up to philosophy to decide which regularities in behaviour and which insights into the structure of the human mind are important, and what kind of epistemology is called for to cover such wide-ranging knowledge. His philosophical position therefore fluctuates considerably, from a revised materialism to Kantianism without a transdencental subject (Ricoeur); a genuine 'structuralist philosophy', however, is not to be found.

Lévi-Strauss's initial experience with philosophy was that it easily sacrificed the observable to the understandable, and vice versa. So he turned away from philosophy, towards the study of concrete patterns of life, towards ethnology. In Indian peoples he recognized an independent rationality, whereas his predecessors such as Lévy-Bruhl could only see a *mentalité primitive*. Influenced by Jakobson, and *via* his continuous debate with cultural anthropologists like Boas, Malinowski, and Mead, Lévi-Strauss once more took up

Frazer's old problem of totemism. He completed these studies in his influential book *Les structures élémentaires de la parenté* (1949) in which the
basic intention to arrive at a 'logical syntaxis of social reality' is already
present. The main argument runs as follows. Man moves from a more-or-less
instinctive level on which he satisfies his needs as an animal, to another level
distinguishable from the first by its regulative character. By ceasing to live
only on the first level, however, man doesn't do away with it: he is at the
same time nature and culture. It is therefore a mistake to see the so-called
primitive communities exclusively as totemistic clans, banded together because of their needs. Even an elementary insight into the difference between
nature and culture, together with this amended view of totemism, casts clear
light on the regulative character of human society. From this stems the view
of kinship systems as (linguistically interpretable) regulative systems. These
basic insights were further elaborated particularly in *La pensée sauvage*
(1962) and in *Anthropologie structurale* (1958).

In what follows, some problems of this kind that may have important
epistemological implications are reviewed.

(i) Among so-called 'savages', we find a science of the concrete which
surpasses our Western knowledge of the concrete. In order to perceive this,
however, we have to be able to view our own system of knowledge in relative
terms. This is difficult to do because the knowledge of the concrete referred
to here can only be understood by us *via* our own means of expression.
Regarded this way, totemistic classifications appear in a quite different light,
i.e. as specific scientific and philosophic achievements. Laws and systems of
transformation are required, especially in transition from one social form to
the other, implying intellectual transformation. Such laws and systems may
be said to constitute a 'language', which can be formalized. Formalization
puts a tool into our hands wherewith to understand realities, and among such
realities may now also be included the science of the concrete as 'savages'
know it.

(ii) We should continue to see the human being as a creator of orders
and ordered events. Lévi-Strauss illustrates this by referring to the names of
individuals. Names relate people in a clearly recognizable way to the struc-
ture-bonded rôle which they play in the classification system. The individual,
in his rôle as individual, receives a specific name.

(iii) All systematizing in human societies is based on something or other
— an axis, as it were, that holds the structure together. The axial unit of the
abstract and the concrete always serves as the basis for the name of the clan.
The same goes for mythologies; they should be studied according to their
form (for instance as a musical form). The observable and the intelligible in

mythologies is taken as concrete and can thus be formalized. But there is structure in the myth as well: the apparent meaning is always different from the real meaning. "Being a sign for something else" does not apply here, but a structure of relationships appears instead, focussed upon the concrete functioning of all other elements.

(iv) For this reason, functionalism is once more in the limelight. One should start with a myth, dissect it as it were into all its elements, and then study its variations, correlations, and transformations as if dealing with the problems of transformation in modern mathematics. This approach implies an assumption about the human sciences, namely that they should observe the same strictness and objectivity as the natural sciences, and should free themselves from the so-called 'human factor'. This factor has manifested itself as a disturbing ideology standing in the way of a more relative approach to knowledge.

(v) The idea of a general scientific model, i.e. of functionalism forming the basis for a theory of the human mind, becomes possible where structures are homologous. Such homologous structures are formed in those manifestations of the human mind where reflexion does not play a major part. Linguistics, cultural anthropology, and psychoanalysis nowadays form a methodological triangle which usurps the rôle of former, time-honoured, principles in the human sciences. What is of philosophical and epistemological interest here is that this triangle can, by means of a constructed and constructable holistic model, influence all meaningful human action. Moreover, this rests on the assumption that the structures of the understandable and of the concrete are, in the last analysis, identical. Since Mauthner and Wittgenstein, this insight has not only significantly inspired present-day philosophy of language, but it was also taken up by other philosophical disciplines. The principle underlying it departs from idealistic and dialectic convictions about thought and world being identical. Lévi-Strauss's conviction is different: that which separates thought from the world, and intelligibility from reality, is mathematical in nature. *La pensée sauvage* presents the human mind as a reservoir of combinations, permutations, and similar processes, which may all be regarded as mathematical. This reservoir is an almost inexhaustible source of possible structures. The world, says Lévi-Strauss, has never had sufficient meaning attached to it, and thought has always had a considerable surplus of opportunities at its disposal to designate the concrete and to invest it with meaning. In this perennial surplus, meanings are allocated by means of symbols, i.e. in conformity with the laws of thought. No model ever conceived is completely arbitrary: 'the nature of the thing' is always relevant.

(vi) We should add to these arguments that our epistemological model has been historically developed and can hardly be said to be relativistic. Nevertheless, according to Lévi-Strauss, man has no claim to a privileged place in the universe and in the totality of history, and the same goes for Occidental human beings who have created the genetic and evolutionary models of history. It is therefore a mistake which Sartre for instance makes to maintain that Lévi-Strauss rejects history. He rejects only that model of history which produced twentieth-century Occidental hegemony, and considers this as being history's final achievement. We have here a counter to Hegel: in some form or other, Hegel's logic of progress keeps cropping up in approaches to history. "Western civilization seems to be the most progressive expression of the development of human societies. Primitive groups accordingly rank as 'remnants' of earlier stages. Accordingly, if they are to be classified logically, the classification should at the same time indicate their chronological order." (*4.34*, 13) This is the grossest of errors, brought about by equally serious confusion of value judgments which can never be universally valid. History thus acquires new relevance in the fields of epistemology and of relativist philosophy, the position of the observer vis-à-vis his object being fundamentally important. Lévi-Strauss believes that the structuralist method, *via* arguments set out above, can lead to a system of relations which is *independent* of both at one and the same time, i.e. independent of the observer and independent of the object. We, however, agree with Fleischmann: Structual anthropology also does not succeed in finding this Archimedic point (which would in any case have been incompatible with its own functionalism) but it may have succeeded in building a system of relations that is at one and the same time *dependent* upon both the observer and his object. (*4.42*, 108)

This difference between *dependence* and *independence* is epistemologically relevant, and is to a considerable extent decisive of the fortunes of structuralism. In order to understand this, one should read the introductory chapter to *Anthropologie structurale,* which deals with history and ethnology. Lévi-Strauss sees every society as an ensemble of symbolic systems; language, matrimonial rules, and mutual relationships between art, science, religion, etc. The dynamics of that ensemble are governed by two principles: contradiction and mutation. A society either collapses because of its contradictions (for instance through inner contradictions within a system or through incommensurability of different systems) or it finds itself in a condition of constant mutation. Here too there is a parallel with linguistics. Both contradiction and mutation stem either from infrastructures that are independent of the human mind (such as changes in the natural environment) or from the human mind itself. If from the latter, then light is cast upon the necessarily twofold meaning contained in the concept of structure: structure involves intelligibility as well as reality. Once we accept the human capacity to understand as a basic cause for the concept of structure, then it must at the same time be considered as *causa efficiens*. This conclusion has its consequences concerning the objectivity of the structure, and concerning the implicit scientific concept of structural thought (*14*, 0.9). As soon as the elements of a structure no longer function independently of their articulation within the structure as a whole, one can no longer maintain that their mutual relationships are objective data. The complex as a whole then becomes dependent upon the subjective agent who attributes meaning to it. Even when one knows quite well that the elements in the structure cannot be viewed in isolation from one another, one nevertheless should try to formulate objective definitions. Otherwise, the network of elements and relations would not correctly represent reality. It is ultimately on this kind of objectivity that the possibility of a universal — highly formalized — language, which could symbolize any concept, is based. Even this implies, not independence but *complete dependence*, of the observer and the observed object. Lévi-Strauss refers in this regard to the epistemological implications that arise when the structure is seen as a model. This is especially to be found in his essay on the structural concept of ethnology, which is the heart of the epistemology in the *Anthropologie structurale.* Lévi-Strauss's philosophical ideas may be stated in the single lapidary sentence: "... finally, the model must be constructed in such a way that it can allow for all established facts ..." (*4.34*, 302) He thus seeks to introduce order into the world, *without* answering the question whether this is an intelligible order only, or whether it also involves reality. This question requires an answer, and should not be lost sight of amid the wealth of Lévi-Strauss's impressive cultural anthropological material. We should not forget that the world *is* not a structure, nor should we forget that intelligibility goes beyond each conceptualization. This fact is denied by the idea of independence, and confirmed by the idea of dependence. In both cases, philosophical questions, however, remain unanswered.

3. PHILOSOPHICAL DESIGNS

A genuine structuralist philosophy is to be found neither with Lévi-Strauss nor in more recent hermeneutics. Still less is it to be found in literary criticism, or in the psychoanalysis of the structuralist *milieux*. Theses which have since the Moscow formalists become generalities in Western literary criticism, linguistics, cultural anthropology, and psychology are approached anew, and often placed in new perspective; but the philosophical implications of such themes have hardly become any clearer. On the contrary, there is a vacillating uncertainty about the resultant wealth of linguistic, anthropological, and psychological material, the scientific value of which is not self-evident. It is particularly such basic philosophical problems as the epistemological one, (viz. intelligibility and reality, thinking and world, language and reality) that are vague; and this problem is connected with the general question whether philosophy as such is indeed possible. One hears so much nowadays about the 'death' of philosophy. Even the more specific designs which structuralist *milieux* have given birth to do not open the way to a consistent philosophical structuralism, but limit themselves to the general aspects of structuralist philosophizing. This goes for the Paris philosopher Jacques Derrida, but also applies to Michel Foucault and even to Louis Althusser, important interpreter of Marx.

A. *Grammatology*

Jacques Derrida, head of the philosophical department of the *École Normale Supérieure,* is particularly interested in basic principles and methods of philosophizing. The important and complicated works he has published since 1959 have been built up out of slowly evolving comments on Plato, Hegel, Freud, Husserl, Lévi-Strauss, and Levinas. From these, the question as to whether philosophy itself is possible has taken shape, especially in the form of the basic problem as to whether there is any such thing as metaphysics. Derrida's basic argument is founded on the statement that philosophy is rooted in the Greek and Western *episteme* (meaning), i.e. in the history of *logos.* The *telos* of all Western philosophy is determined by logicality; logicality may be discovered in every philosophical *discours*, appearing both as its result and its underlying assumption. According to Derrida, this logocentric thinking has to be abandoned, so that its place may be taken by grammatological thinking, outdistancing philosophical logology and its specific presuppositions.

Any philosophical term is related to other concepts. Thus a specific system of concepts and relations arises, which, however, is difficult to define in exact terms. Derrida proves, in his commentaries on Husserl (*La forme et le vouloir-dire,* 1967; *La voix et le phénoméne,*1967), that even the concept of 'form', so important to Husserl, is part of a context which also includes concepts such as: sense, evidence, essence, truth, the present. This structure should be seen as an interplay of relations, oppositions, and differences — reminders of Wittgenstein's theory of speech and of family likeness

of meanings are combined with de Saussure's differentialism. This interplay can be understood on the basis of the metaphysical-ontologi-
cal idea of *logos*. One's form of thinking makes one conceive reality as the
neuter of the present: it is. Phenomenology is thinking of being as an 'it is',
which is metaphysical. The same holds for de Saussure. Just as Husserl distinguishes between *sense* and *meaning* and separates the two (*Logische Untersuchungen*, II, 1) whilst they are basically inter-connected, so for de Saussure *signifiant* is separated from *signifié* — although they too are basically
inseparable. Derrida holds it against de Saussure that he detaches these two
concepts from their context, setting them up as independent, and so postu-
lating a relatively closed system of speech. The way he does this is, however,
arbitrary, and provides no justification for us to accept any priorities what-
soever. De Saussure goes even further when he identifies *signifié* with intelligibility, making the concept independent from *signifiant*. In so far as de
Saussure actually applies his arbitrary and differentialist approach to the
signifié only, and not to the total sign which includes both *le signifiant* and
le signifié, he lays himself open to the charge of being limited by metaphysical
prejudices. Another objection should be raised: de Saussure's linguistics is
basically one of the spoken word, the written word being considered of
secondary importance. This fact should not be understood solely in terms of
Western linguistic tradition. It is also connected with the idea that a spoken
word is more adequate in conveying meaning than a written one. Seen from
this point of view, the voice is consciousness itself. When I speak, I am not
only conscious of being present at what I think, I am also as near as possible
to my thought. Derrida remarks that a 'transcendental appearance' is thus
brought about, in which *le signifiant* seems to become transparent, and in
which the concept manifests itself as though it were the autonomous present.
This is, however, in appearance only: the sign is indivisible, the conceptual
cannot become independent, the language is a formal game of oppositions
and differences *(différences)*. Every sign therefore is a *trace*, always referring
to other signs, and never understandable if it is thought of as being autar-
chical. Consequently, there can be no single elements on their own, but only
those traces which always refer us to further traces. This has at least two
consequences. In the first place, functionalism in this philosophy has been
transformed into a philosophy of relationships without elements — a philosophy thus in which there is nothing but reference to other references or
frames of reference. The functionalist components of structuralist thinking
may be said to have been carried to absurdity. In the second place, the subject is also taken up into this pattern of references — is caught in the specific
system of signs — which precedes speaking and writing. The subject can only

speak in so far as it follows the traces of the grammata of the writing
(écriture).

This criticism of de Saussure and the idea of a grammatology explains
Derrida's relationships with the *Tel Quel* group. Philippe Sollers's work is to a
considerable extent based on a similar approach. Every text, in this light, is
always a pattern of references to other texts and the transformation of other
texts. (This point of view is also Roland Barthes's in *S/Z*.) Thus neither the
autonomous creative subject nor a purely original text exists. Grammatology
is the positive science of the textuality (Kristeva speaks of *intertextualité*),
of the grammata, and the original writ. They all dictate how we should write
and how we should speak. With this insight we should be liberated from
logocentrism.

The question how this game of differences (in de Saussure's sense) is
possible is associated with the question of whether philosophy itself is possible. Derrida draws further conclusions in his contribution to the *Tel Quel*
theory (*4.1*). The thoughts outlined above lead to the question of differences
as a difference (*la différAnce*). This *differAnce* cannot be presented as an
'it is', because it is inconceivable as form, as sign, as being. One would land
right back in onto-theological metaphysics if this were not true. One would
have to be *outside* this metaphysics and its structure of concepts to discover
the origin of the *différAnce*. But the concept of origin itself, and that of
outside, already belongs to this metaphysics. How does one break out of this
circle? Derrida says we can only repeat the metaphysical text in such a way
that the circle is elongated into an ellipse. The philosophy which seeks to go
back to origins, which has to prove itself by being logical, which has a *telos*,
which accepts a transcendental truth as the final outcome of its activities —
such a philosophy would be shaken to its foundation as soon as the circle
began to be expanded. Thus a philosophical strategy is called for: a repeated
re-reading, a destructive hermeneutics which recognizes the constructive in
its destruction. *DifférAnce* is a game in which the human subject is only a
function.

A comparison with Heidegger suggests itself. Derrida argues that Heidegger was not radical enough in his attack on onto-theological thinking, because
the idea of a history of origin itself ought to have been destroyed. The
concept of a philosophical archaeology (Heidegger, Husserl) has to be supplanted by that of grammatology. The game of *différAnce* is not based on
any ulterior meaning. Derrida's thoughts in this regard are akin to those
of Nietzsche: meaning must be destroyed to make philosophy into a 'joyful'
science: "... and I would not know of anything that the mind of a philosopher would rather be than a good dancer." (*Fröhliche Wissenschaft*, 381)

B. *Archaeology*

Derrida approaches the very boundaries of traditional metaphysics, and there-fore also the boundaries of those aspects of Western philosophy which consider themselves metaphysical. But all thinking about boundaries is think-ing which doesn't permit itself to be thought: that is, about what the boun-dary looks like on this side as well as on the other side. This is what lies be-hind the thought of 'extending the circle'. For Wittgenstein, this problem implies the requirement of silence, a thought we may also find with Derrida. Michel Foucault, on the other hand, whose book *Les mots et les choses* (1966) led him to fame, creates a philosophy of discontinuity – of breaches, shifts, transpositions in history and in epistemology. And he does this so as to provide a contrast with the traditional philosophy of history, which fun-damentally implies a philosophy of identity. He seeks to supplant the egolo-gical nature of thinking about identity by means of archaeology, and hopes in this way to discover the *episteme* of today's thinking from *within* and not from the boundaries. Or, to put it another way, boundaries do not enclose, nor do they present a delimitable field of metaphysics – they are always there as points of cut-off, as thresholds in thinking.

We find topics such as these dealt with in *Folie et déraison* (1961), in *Naissance de la clinique* (1963), and in the study on *Raymond Roussel* (1962). Their principal theme was the historical change in epistemological hypotheses: for instance, a certain social rôle and status is allocated to the mentally disturbed – he is a patient in an institution – thus bringing about the alienation from himself. The eye of the doctor no longer sees a total picture, but only signs, symbols, and structures. In such cases one has to look back: one should practise archaeology in one's own dimen-sion of history so as to understand such changes epistemologically, or as philosophy of history. Thus *Les mots et les choses* includes an epistemology as well as an anthropology. The latter, whose central theme is *'la mort de l'homme'*, made the book famous, and popularized it to the extent of bowdlerization. The fundamental theses of the book were detailed and dif-ferentiated in *L'archéologie du savoir* (1969).

Patterns of order exist between words and things *(tableaux, tables, sys-tèmes d'éléments, codes ordinateurs, grilles)* which cement the two together. Science, language, technique, schemes of perception, play such connective rôles. Order is that quality in things which arises from the regularities within the things themselves. This order can only be perceived through the grid of a point of view, or of a language, or of a specific scientific argument. Order is seldom immediately apparent. On the other hand, the fundamental codes

of a culture determine the way in which man enters the empirical
order — the way in which he will live and work, speak and think, and achieve
self-realization. Science and philosophy try to make clear to him why such
an order exists at all, why he obeys its principles, and why it is that *these*
orders rather than others determine his life. Between the order inherent in
in the things themselves and the order induced by the cultural codes lies an
intermediary field, more confused and more difficult to analyse. Between
the eye that has already been codified and the reflexive knowledge, intermediary considerations exist in which order as such is experienced — an anonymous field of knowledge preceding all subjective thinking, speaking, observation, or action. The classical history of ideas did not perceive this field. It
dealt in clear causes and strictly-drawn consequences. The hallmarks of scientific thinking in the eighteenth century are: representation, equality, and
equivalence. Those of the nineteenth century are: origin and continuity. Both
are anthropocentric, which is apparent in the then current views on language,
work, and life. This historical insight calls forth an anthropological counter-
part; either a change in or the end of anthropocentrism — the death of man.
Nietzsche indeed brought the death of man to pass in his fragment, *Der tolle
Mensch*, in which he writes of the Death of God. For the 'mad man' implies the
death of God. With this death, man "rolls from the centre towards X." In our
day, we can only think within the vacuum of 'vanished man'. But this same
vacuum provides space for new possibilities. Anthropology as a universally
valid orientation in thinking disappears before our eyes, and we learn to see
what a drag it was upon our thinking. He who wants to continue to speak of
man, his essence, his access to truth — he who wants to relate all knowledge
to man and who interprets any formalization as an attack on man and his
dignity — such a person merits either a philosophical smile, or no comment.

Foucault, in the many interviews he has meanwhile given, has always argued that his position includes an anti-humanism that represents a complete
dependence on apriority, and that the subject (and implicitly the transcendental consciousness) does not possess its own origins — in short that generality
is more original and more fundamental than the individuality. Any 'transcendental' reflexion is no longer possible, and is incompatible with today's
episteme.

Especially in *L'archéologie du savoir*, thinking in a historical way about
history (which could be described as thinking about identity, as a *discours* of
the continuous), is regarded as a form of egology. Concepts of origin and of
teleology comprise principles of such egology. The idea of consciousness is
central here. Foucault's ideas deviate here from idealism, from phenomenology, and from existentialism. The latter three do not represent

thinking from the *décentrement du sujet*; Marxism and the philosophy of dialogue approach this *episteme*. There is in fact an association with Althusser's interpretations. The philosophy of dialogue is alien to Foucault in the sense that *l'autre* (the other person and the other thing) is anonymous to him, whereas for Levinas, for instance, it is highly concrete. Two components are time and again emphasized by this philosophy: epistemology and anthropology. Marx, Nietzsche, linguistics, and formalism — they all contributed to this change vis-à-vis anthropology, to this anti-anthropology, as it were. The description of all levels of discourse which make scientific and everyday speech and writing possible, and which rule them, is the only remaining task for contemporary thought. The question of possibility is fundamental to Foucault as it is for Derrida. It is connected with, even identical to, *the order of discourse* itself. (*4.53*)

Foucault thus, in the context of structuralism, shifts the accent from the subject to the structure, a process whose beginning may be traced to Russian formalism. Foucault does not, however, evoke a conflict between synchrony and diachrony. He differs here from formalism, but not from the structuralism of the Prague School. On this basis, he discusses a number of historical problems, such as those of mutation and transformation, problems which might indeed be understood in terms of a linguistic model, but which are not themselves linguistic in nature. Thus, with Foucault history enters structuralism's epistemological triangle: linguistics, cultural anthropology, and psychoanalysis. This does not in itself, however, create a structuralist philosophy. Foucault's philosophy seeks, in an analysis of discoursive formations, systems of statements which exhibit a certain regularity. In these systems, which are also found in science, philosophy, the arts and literature, we find the following elements: objects that could be defined by such systems, typologies of statement, applied principles, and the theories and themes that function in the relevant systems. These are to be found neither in the subject of the discourse nor in its formal laws and regularities, but in its general progress.

C. *Marxism*

In neither Russian formalism nor Czech structuralism was there clear differentiation between the concepts of function, structure, and system. Neither did the debate with Marxism create such a differentiation — this debate remained no more than an exchange between a formalist functional approach or a structuralist approach on the one hand, and the Marxist approach on the other. More fundamental definition and differentiation grew out of confrontation with theory of information and with cybernetics, (*5.1*) not from within

the content of structuralist discussions on their own. The Marxist approach
is actually nearer to functionalism than to structuralism. Functionalist thinking after all never moves very far from the immediate vicinity of social reality. Functions are deduced from human action, but structures cannot be.
Structures, unlike functions, cannot be understood on the level of language
as it is actually spoken, but must be understood on the level of syntax and
semantics. The logicality of the structure and the functionality of the function jointly make up one system.

Marxism's first concerns with these problems are therefore to be interpreted in a functionalist, not in a structuralist, sense. Joseph Stalin's well-known
Pravda letters on *Marxism and Problems of Linguistics,* 1950 *(4.66)*, which
were directed against the ideas of Marr, opened up the way towards a non-
dogmatic linguistics: language does not belong to the superstructure, but is
generally to be seen as an instrument. The instrumentality and the universa-
lity of language are emphasized; the ordering of language after all influences
every social reality. Although Stalin admits that the evolution of language
may follow a functionalist model, his own concept of that evolution remains
organismic: neologisms are created, old elements of the language die. Words
are for Stalin the basic elements of a system of language; the structure of
language is built up out of words and grammar. With this as background, we
should note that the first reconciliatory approach between Marxist and structuralist thinking was effected *via* the functionalism they have in common
(2.1). For they agree that order in social life can be demonstrated with the
aid of linguistics. Marxism tries to study the essential properties, structuralism
the formal properties of this order.

Louis Althusser, a teacher at the *École Normale Supérieure,* sets out to
interpret Marxism in a structuralist *milieu.* In the first place, he tries, like
Lacan and Foucault, to justify Marxist thinking on scientific grounds and to
give it a philosophic interpretation. This raises two sets of epistemological
problems. According to Althusser, Marx is to be seen both as the creator of
a theory of history and as a philosopher. If one is to understand all of this
properly, one has to re-read Marx from a structuralist perspective. *(Lire
le Capital,* 1965). We find the same methodological orientation again
in *Pour Marx* (1968). The spoken or written language, the language
on whose level the functionalist re-orientation and the breakthrough
took place, forms a structure. Yet there is another structure as well. This is
what Althusser wants to reveal. Every text has two dimensions. The directly
deducible dimension is itself structured by another dimension. There are
after all questions, considerations, other texts *(intertextualité),* and situations
which determine the author just as much as they determine the text which

is finally put down on paper. This means that reading on both levels is essential, and is epistemologically highly relevant: in this way, a *lecture épistémologique* is created. By a reading of this kind, we arrive at an insight into Marx's works which, according to Althusser, is characterized by humanist, ideological, and pre-scientific thinking about history, politics, and economics, but at the same time it also causes us to break with such thinking, which is the very way in which we develop a scientific attitude towards such questions. Althusser dates the break as following upon 1848, i.e. after *Die heilige Familie* (The Holy Family) and *Die deutsche Ideologie* (The German Ideology). Economics has come to be regarded as an autonomous element within the social structure; and functions as a structure within a more comprehensive totality of structures. It is no longer a matter of people or groups of people; subjects are no longer the real object of economics. Instead, a theory arises that there are elements without subjects, and a study arises of the mutual relations of these elements within one and the same structural context. So once again we encounter the problem which we have already met in Russian formalist aesthetics, in Czech structuralism, and in Lacan and Foucault, viz. that structuralist opinions are incompatible with any rôle of the autonomously constitutive subject in a philosophically idealist sense. Thought which concerns itself with the essence of things (*Wesensdenken*) always is accompanied by an empirical conception of the subject. Structuralism, on the other hand, inevitably leads to the *décentrement* of the subject. Marx indeed provides us with a number of notes and annotations in which the two views are simultaneously parallel and juxtaposed to one another. Althusser regards this reading of Marx as being closely related to Foucault's problem of humanism. But he also finds anti-humanism in Marx. Indeed, without this two-sidedness Marxism could not be regarded as scientific. Thus the structuralist problem is no longer contrasted with Marxism; the problem instead becomes one of structural thinking *within* Marxism. This is important, since the interpretation, according to which the relationship between structuralism and Marxism consists in a confrontation between the two, is false. Actually, the question lies within one and the same ideology, i.e. Marxism.

The Prague Circle developed a consistent theory concerning the relationships between the aesthetic object and society. It dealt with the rôle of the subject, with a new hermeneutics, and with a theory of innovation. French structuralism, by and large, did not take the matter any further, especially in its interpretation of Marx. Efforts to interpret historical-dialectical materialism of *practice* as if it were based on the anti-humanism of Foucault and Althusser have thus far been relatively unsuccessful. This is admitted by Kosik in his book *Dialektik des Konkreten* (1967). Since publication of his

Critique de la raison dialectique (1960), Sartre has appeared as the critical observer here. He notes that this lack of success could not be otherwise, since the theory of anti-humanism could never manage to mediate between subject and practice. This mediation according to him is the actual problem to be dealt with in this context.

> The method of science is analytical – that of philosophy can only be dialectical. Philosophy questions practice, and thus of course man, for he is the totalizing subject of history. Whether that subject is decentred or not is of no importance. The heart of the matter is not what has been made out of man, but what man himself makes out of that which has been made out of him. What has been made out of man are the structures, the units of meaning, which comprise the study of the human and social sciences. What man makes is history itself, the transcendence of these structures in a totalizing practice. Philosophy mediates between the two. Practice, in its operation, is a complete totalization; but it always boils down to an incomplete totalization which in turn is transcended. The philosopher thus is he who tries to think this transcendence.

Marxism serves to present us, not with a fixed system, but with a task in hand, a design to be executed. The same problem of mediation appears where the subject is concerned. "One has to understand how the subject or subjectivity constructs itself on a basis that is given it, and by means of a continuous process of internalization and renewed externalization." (*4.63*, 132ff.)

To what extent does practice succeed in fulfilling its mediatory rôle? Althusser, unlike Foucault, considers that there is room for humanism, because it is connected with practice. Humanism, as an ideology, is concrete practice with a specific structure, functioning within more comprehensive structures. Humanism as a practice should serve to combat any form of discrimination and should promote the transition of the dictatorship of the proletariat into Communism. The ideology of humanism therefore has become political, but at the same time it has also become a category of history: it fulfils an important rôle in Marx's historical transformations.

Althusser therefore conceives of history as a humanized ideology, as practice. An anti-humanist anthropology is in that case both impossible and unnecessary, for practice and political activity for the most part overlap. There is, however, still a residual ambiguity. This becomes clear when we discuss changes in the direction of Communism. The ambiguity can be seen *in the interpretation of history*. When the structurally-oriented Marxists speak of history, they speak of it as a history of thinking about the origin and the essence of phenomena (*Wesensdenken*), history that is an ensemble of phenomena that are freely determinable. The same question that Lévi-Strauss asked arises here. Is there a *single* history which can take care of the sum total of human genesis, or are there only autonomous histories, which have to be

understood by means of structuralist thinking according to certain fundamental rules? If the latter, we once more end up with a game of order, in
which human order is virtually always present.

This ambiguity, inherent in Marxism, is also found in Western thinking that is not Marxist. Lévi-Strauss has not shied away from bringing this
ambiguity into the open. Can Marxism mediate, when it itself contains this
ambiguity? When the problem of practice is carried into politics, it serves
only to lead us away from this fundamental question: practice as a concrete
philosophy of thinking about *ordo* could, however, lead us directly to this
problem. Only in this way could structuralism be a humanism that unmasks
humanism. "My humanity," says Nietzsche in *Ecce Homo,* "is a constant
victory over myself."

CHAPTER V

WHAT IS STRUCTURALISTIC PHILOSOPHIZING?

We have hitherto been emphasizing that an independent structuralistic philosophy does not exist. Structuralism is not a new philosophy, nor is it a philosophical movement comparable to existentialism or phenomenology. Fashionable writers in literary journals might like this to be the case, but from a philosophical point of view there is no support for it. It is only the fashion of the day which makes us believe that one philosophical movement has taken the place of another. It is today's fashion which proclaims Paris structuralism *dernier cri*. In fact, many so-called structuralist authors like Lucien Goldmann argue that the concept of structure has long been at home in the intellectual life of France. French cubism, the contemporary of Russian formalism, illustrates this. The concept of structure lies at the root of important developments in the scientific and philosophical thinking of our century, roots that go far too deep for structuralism to be facilely presented as being 'today's thing.'

By saying this, however, we do not answer the question what structuralistic philosophizing really means. Any effort to answer this question should bear two aspects in mind. On the one hand, following Roland Barthes, we have structuralistic activity. This implies, where our problem is concerned, that *philosophizing may itself be a structuralist activity*, whatever this activity might turn out to be. On the other hand, we may regard a philosophy of structuralism *as a philosophy*, in which case the question of a structuralist activity, and the conditions for it, become most important. Only if we wish to consider both these two aspects can we really take up the question: What is structuralistic philosophizing?

1. SERIES

Roland Barthes, as we have already said, limits structuralism to structuralist activity. This has a two-fold meaning. Firstly, we must from the start regard as relative all opinions that insist on a firm philosophical standpoint, i.e. a *corpus* of scientific or philosophical knowledge. Secondly, we may regard structuralism itself as an activity that is concerned, not only with knowing, but also with doing. We have already repeatedly argued that this activity consists mainly of two typical operations: arrangement and analysis. These are however, not goals in themselves but determine the goal that Foucault,

Barthes, and many others have stated as the goal of structuralist activity, namely to *evoke new objects*. This goal in its turn has two aspects: a constructive and a reconstructive aspect. These can be distinguished from one another but never separated from one another. The constructive aspect is the more important in structuralistically-oriented aesthetics (the pioneering work of French cubism and Russian constructivism are examples). The reconstructive aspect is more apparent in philosophical reflexions upon such aesthetics. Structuralist activity tries to reconstruct an object in such a way that the rules according to which it functions are demonstrated. The structure thus exposed becomes the *simulacrum* of the object. In the frontier zone between what is given as a given given and as a reconstructed given we find the intelligible. This 'intelligible', especially in the form of technical intelligibility, is regarded by the structuralist thinkers as the essence of every human creation. In so far as the constructive and reconstructive act are inalienably linked together (the latter often is an 'eidetic' activity in Husserl's phenomenological sense) there is no fundamental difference between philosophy on the one hand and art, literature, or science on the other. This enables Foucault to say that he thinks that philosophy just doesn't exist any more. Not that it has disappeared, but that it has been split up into a great many different activities. Thus the work of the linguist, the historian, the poet, the revolutionary, can all be forms of philosophical activity. Whereas what was philosophical in the nineteenth century was to be found in reflexions upon the conditions on which the object was possible, philosophy nowadays (according to Foucault) is any activity which presents the object in a new light — whether in practice or epistemologically. It doesn't matter whether this activity is considered to belong to mathematics, linguistics, ethnology, or history.

The question becomes more difficult when one tries to state what contribution the philosophy of structuralism can make when regarded as philosophy. One would then have to determine the possibility of, and the conditions for, the activity described above; and would in addition have to determine what the specifically philosophical aspect of that was. Philosophical questions then appear with profiles that are difficult to define. In the early stage of our argument we mentioned that the concept of structure has many facets and is often diffuse. The same goes for other philosophical themes in structuralist thinking, such as consciousness, truth, achievement, system, subject, *signifiant, signifié*. Different writers often use them as they see fit, which does not result in a uniform picture which could then be subjected to philosophical reflexions. The divergence in the philosophical designs of the structuralist groups we have discussed (such as those of Derrida, Foucault, and Althusser) prove this. These writers run the risk of observing everything in the perspective of one principle only: everything becomes *trace,* everything becomes *discours,* everything becomes practice.

This observation would be virtually shattering to a logocentric philosophy (to borrow Derrida's term). For various reasons, however, structuralist writers have tried to state logocentric philosophy in relative terms. The profile of philosophical problems simply cannot any longer be defined in the vocabulary hitherto employed, nor in the current logicity. These are, at the most, certain series of philosophical problem-complexes which are important for structuralism. These series must possess at one and the same time common and distinctive properties, just like Mondriaan's squares show affinity by their form, but at the same time show differences in colour and proportions. Changes in these series, which are indeed brought about in the various constructive and reconstructive structuralist activities, immediately produce a change in the whole. In this way, according to the linguistic principles of de Saussure, the implicit philosophical problems acquire their significative existence by their boundaries, by delimitations as actual or even as potential elements within a philosophical problem-complex. No longer is it only the contents of the problem-complexes that are important, but also their position in a series, and the position of that series in the whole structure. This system is fundamentally an open one. New series can always replace or supplement those already in existence. In this connexion, the discussion on the content and the use of basic concepts in philosophy acquires new meaning, and this applies particularly to the concept of structure.

In structuralist theory, various series can be distinguished, all playing a part in present-day philosophical approaches, though on different epistemological levels. Without claiming to be complete, we mention some of these.

episteme	/	subjectivity	/	history	
structure	/	function	/	system	
relativism	/	positivism metaphysics	/	scientificism	

science	/	aesthetics	/	philosophy	/ mysticism
$\dfrac{\text{knowledge}}{\text{experience}}$	/	$\dfrac{\text{knowledge}}{\text{reflexion}}$	/	$\dfrac{\text{knowledge}}{\text{verification}}$	
$\dfrac{\text{structure}}{\text{essence}}$	/	$\dfrac{\text{structure}}{\text{scheme}}$	/	$\dfrac{\text{sense}}{\text{meaning}}$	

This and similar series, becoming individually more and more complex, function in various structuralist positions. They ought to be brought together in a matrix, so that they may be read, not only horizontally, but also vertically and diagonally. The contrasting implications or breaks, shifts, or changes in the matrix could then be analysed functionally. With the aid of the resultant 'philosophical mobile', a structuralistic philosophy ought to develop as a structuralist activity.

2. ORDO

These observations are 'playful' in more senses of the word than one. They show, however, that structuralism is not to be characterized by the content or the interpretation of certain philosophical concepts, but by the activity which may be developed from such concepts and their content.

A far-reaching conclusion follows from this. Structuralism, especially when conceived as a philosophical activity, is responsible for *the problem of order becoming the object of philosophy*. The problem of order no longer is considered the foundation of philosophy, as it used to be in for instance the more ancient, ontologically-oriented *cosmologia rationalis.*

In the aesthetics of our century, this has already clearly been applied, especially in cubism, formalism, and constructivism. Thus many elements of artistic and aesthetic activities can be fitted in with the philosophical views on structuralism. The work of art is not created according to a prescribed order — it is the order itself which creates the work.

The essential nature of art is in this case defined by the concept of order, the objective of art is equated with the objective of any activity that creates order. Indeed, the aesthetic effect itself is to be experienced as an ordering. This need not surprise us. Any aesthetic reality is a victory over chaos, it testifies as to the legitimacy of the work of art: the work of art, being there, *has* to be as it is and has to be *such* as it is. Otherwise it is mere chaos, or some other work of art.

This thought forms the background of a widespread formalism, which formalism is connected with the significant fact that concepts like 'organization', 'montage', and 'arrangement' are so current in our century, and are used to describe works of art. This applies not only to Roland Barthes or the Russian formalists, but also to Klee, Kandinsky, Eisenstein, Le Corbusier, and Thomas Mann, as well as to Webern, Stravinsky, and Stockhausen. Rilke expresses the difficulty in no longer creating art within the structure of a prescribed order but by means of a putting into order in a letter he wrote in 1917 in which he speaks of Picasso's 'analytical art', "I should like to know a great painter who — as seems to be the case with Picasso — went through cubism

under his own steam. Only he would be capable of offering us the complete
key to Cézanne's immense, heroic, and desperate work, namely the attempt to
emancipate all the elements in a painting by maintaining an indifference
to the concreteness of the things portrayed. One can hardly believe the extent to which the painter is influenced by predispositions that cling to the
subject. Madonna and apple are equivalent, but in a hundred details the
content nevertheless prevails." This last sentence illustrates the inner struggle
not only to attain the formalist point of view but also to realize the aesthetic problems of the *ordo*.

All these considerations and these data may be applied to philosophical
problems *stricto sensu*. The connexion between structure and *ordo* is the
theme of the transition from a classical ontological cosmology to a cosmology
in which, because of the emancipation from one particular order, the general
theme of order may indeed actually become the theme. In classical cosmology
being is interpreted as BEING. The 'world' theme of order, implicit in
BEING, i.e. that all that exists is interconnected, was of necessity neglected.
The definite change could come about as soon as this theme was emancipated.
This is clear from the three classical efforts that were making progress
in developing the theme of order in the direction we described. (5.7, 51ff.)
The first of these efforts is that of the *cosmologia rationalis* with as its main
theme *nexus et connexum*. The second effort may be found in the transcendental logic of Kant's *Kritik der reinen Vernunft*, with as its main theme
uniformity and inclusion (*Einstimmigkeit und Enthaltensein*). The third
effort comes from Hegel's *Logik* with 'something and something else' (*Etwas
und Anderes*) as the main theme.

This 'something' (in structuralism such 'something' would be called 'element') would not, in classical cosmology, be regarded as *ens*, but as *res in
serie rerum* or *in rerum nexu*. This emphasizes the universal interconnexions
of determinants. The interconnexions are, however, governed by their basic
laws *principia identatis, contradictionis, exclusii tertii,* and *principium rationis
sufficientis*, so that the theme of order is not rendered independent.

In Kant's 'pure' and 'formal' logic, the theme of *ordo* still is ontological,
but in his transcendental logic changes seem to appear, particularly
in connexion with the concept of possibility. For Kant, after all,
distinguishes between a real, a logical, and a transcendental concept
of possibility. If one transposes this thought into the 'world' theme, we find
this difference described by Kant in a letter to Reinhold in 1789. "...The
Divine Will is something, the existent world is something entirely different.
And yet the one is supposed to produce the other." And so Kant rejects the
tradition of Leibnitz-Wolff, which involved taking theology and ontology

out of the traditional cosmological theme of order. The theme of uniformity and inclusion (*Kritik der reinen Vernunft*, B628) is also relevant in this connexion. 'Possibility', according to B628, means: conformity with the general conditions applying in any case to possible empirical knowledge. This is not at all identical with the concept of inclusion, which is applied to the context of total experience. The distinction would, however, be meaningless within the context of traditional cosmology — there the already mentioned principle would also have been the highest basic principle applying to all synthetic postulates. This view bases the concept of possibility not only on uniformity, but, according to B628, also on its inclusion in the context of total experience, i.e. the 'world' theme. This represents a considerable emancipation of the theme of order.

In Hegel's logic, too, the 'something' has not been defined in *rerum nexu* but as an independent constituent element in a network of interrelationships. The problem of interrelationship as a problem of *ordo* claims our attention in the form of an interrelationship between something and something else. This problem is more important than the problem of the something in itself — 'somethings' fundamentally belong together. The emphasis of this logic is not on the question of identity and contradiction but on the problem of the categorical entanglement of these 'somethings'. (*5.2*)

In this way, the theme of order has become the object of Western philosophy. In our century, an extra-philosophical triangle, highly relevant to epistemology, has been created: linguistics, cultural anthropology, and psychoanalysis. In this triangle, the question of order is once more raised: it is the central theme in structuralistic thinking. In so far as philosophizing is possible as a structuralist activity, it is part of the task of this activity to expand the developments of the problem of order, as outlined above, and to combine them in one synthesizing context. This would probably be the most important 'series' for structuralistic philosophizing, and at the same time the most important breach of the *episteme*. In so far as there is a philosophy (or theory) of this activity, it questions the conditions of this combination, either from the boundaries (as Derrida does) or from the centre (as Foucault does). Structuralistic philosophizing involves at the same time the practice of the series and the philosophy of the order.

BIBLIOGRAPHY

The bibliography does not claim to be complete; it contains only the most important works that are closely connected with the text. Russian and Czech titles have been translated into English. French, Dutch and German titles appear in their original languages. (In the text itself, the English version of many titles appears as well.)

DISPOSITION

0. INTRODUCTORY WORKS AND SURVEYS

A. *Structuralism*

0.1   Auzias, J.M., *Clefs pour le structuralisme,* Paris 1967.
0.2   Bierwisch, M., 'Strukturalismus. Geschichte, Probleme und Methoden', *Kursbuch* **V** (1966).
0.3   Ducrot, O., Todorov, T., Sperber, D., Safouan, M., Wahl, F., *Qu'est-ce que le structuralisme?,* Paris 1968.
0.4   Ehrmann, J. (ed.), *Structuralism,* Yale French Studies, 1966 (Translations and essays on French structuralism, with bibliography and commentary up to 1965).
0.5   *Esprit,* Nov. 1963, 'La pensée sauvage et le structuralisme'.
0.6   *Esprit,* May 1967, 'Structuralisme, idéologie et méthode'.
0.7   Fages, J.B., *Comprendre le structuralisme,* Paris 1967.
0.8   Gallas, H. (ed.), 'Strukturalismusdiskussion', *Alternative* (1967) No. 54.
0.9   Parain-Vial, J., *Analyses structurales et ideologies structuralistes,* Paris 1969.
0.10 Peperzak, A., 'Denken in Parijs', *Algemeen Nederlands Tijdschrift voor Wijsbegeerte* **LXII**, 3(1970).
0.11 Piaget, J., *Le structuralisme,* Paris 1968.

0.12 Schiwy, G., *Der französische Strukturalismus* (mit einem Textanhang), Hamburg 1969.
0.13 *Tel Quel*, 1966, No. 26, 'Linguistique, psychanalyse, litterature'.
0.14 *Temps Modernes, Les*, Nov. 1966, 'Problèmes du structuralisme'.

B. Linguistics

0.15 *Alternative*, 1969, No. 65, 'Sprachwissenschaft und Literatur'.
0.16 Benveniste, E., *Problèmes de linguistique générale*, Paris 1966.
0.17 Chomsky, N., *Syntactic structures*, Den Haag 1968.
0.18 Jakobson, R., 'Linguistics', in *Main Trends of Research in the Social and Human Sciences* Vol. 1, UNESCO/Mouton, Den Haag 1970.
0.19 Jakobson, R., *Essais de linguistique générale*, Paris 1963 (translated from the English, with an extensive introduction by N. Ruwet).
0.20 Malmberg, B., *Structural Linguistics and Human Communication*, Heidelberg 1963.
0.21 Martinet, A., *Eléments de linguistique générale*, Paris 1960.
0.22 Saussure, F. de, *Cours de linguistique générale*, Paris 1915.
0.23 Trubetzkoy, N.S., *Fundamentals of Phonology*, Prague 1939.
0.001 Dijk, T.A. Van, *Taal, Tekst, Teken*, Amsterdam 1970.
0.002 Maatje, F.C., *Literatuurwetenschap*, Utrecht 1970.
0.003 Šaumjan, S., *Structural Linguistics*, München 1971.

1. TERMINOLOGICAL AND SOCIOLOGICAL POSITION

1.1 Améry, F., 'Französische Sozialphilosophie im Zeichen der 'linken Frustration', *Merkur* (1966), No. 215.
1.2 Bastide, R. (ed.), *Sens et usage du terme structure dans les sciences humaines et sociales*, Den Haag, 1962.
1.3 Bertalanffy, L. von, *Das Biologische Weltbild*, Bern 1948.
1.4 Boudon, R., *A quoi sert la notion de 'structure'?*, Paris 1968.
1.5 Furet, F., 'Les Français et le structuralisme', *Preuves*, No. 192.
1.6 Jaeggi, U., *Ordnung und Chaos*, Frankfurt 1968.
1.7 Kahnweiler, D.H., *Juan Gris*, Paris 1946.
1.8 Kroeber, A.L., *Anthropology*, New York 1948.
1.9 Mouloud, N., *Les structures*, Paris 1968.
1.10 Viet, J., *Les méthodes structuralistes dans les sciences sociales*, Den Haag 1965.
1.11 Wieser, W., *Organismen, Strukturen, Maschinen*, Frankfurt 1959.

2. RUSSIAN FORMALISM

2.1 Broekman, Jan M., 'Russisch formalisme, Marxisme, Strukturalisme', *Tijdschrift voor Filosofie* **XXXXII**, 1 (1971).
2.2 Eichenbaum, B., *Aufsätze zur Theorie und Geschichte der Literatur*, Frankfurt 1965.
2.3 Erlich, V., *Russian Formalism*, Den Haag 1955. (There are several translations of this work. It has an extensive bibliography, which does not appear in all translations. For this bibliography, see the German translation, München 1964).
2.4 Grebenickovà, R., 'Moderner Roman und russische formale Schule', *Alternative* (1966) No. 47.
2.5 Jakobson, R., 'Un exemple de migration de termes et de modèles institutionnels', *Tel Quel* (1970) 41.
2.6 L'Hermite, R. (ed.), 'La linguistique en U.R.S.S.', special issue of the periodical *Languages*, Paris 1969.

2.7   Jauss, H.R., *Literaturgeschichte als Provokation der Literaturwissenschaft*, Konstanz 1967.
2.8   Lichatschow, D., *Nach dem Formalismus*, München 1968.
2.9   Propp, V., *Morphologie du conte*, Paris 1965 (first complete translation).
2.10   Striedter, J. (ed.), *Texte der russischen Formalisten*, Vol. 1, Munchen 1969 (with an introduction by the editor: 'Zur formalistischen Theorie der Prosa und der literarischen Evolution'), and Stempel, W.D. (ed.), *Texte der Russischen Formalisten*, Vol. 2, München 1972.
2.11   Striedter, J., 'Transparenz und Verfremdung', in: *Immanente Aesthetik, Aesthetische Reflexion*, München 1966.
2.12   Todorov, T., 'Théorie de la littérature. Textes des formalistes russes', *Collection Tel Quel*, Paris 1965.
2.13   Trotzki, L., *Literature and Revolution*, 1924 (Russian edition).
2.14   Tschizewsky, D., 'Wiedergeburt des Formalismus? In welcher Art?' in: *Immanente Aesthetik, Aesthetische Reflexion*, München 1966.
2.15   Tynjanov, J., *Die literarischen Kunstmittel und die Evolution in der Literatur*, Frankfurt 1967.
2.16   Tynjanov, J. and Jakobson, R., 'Probleme der Literatur- und Sprachforschung', 1928, *Kursbuch V (1966)*.
2.17   Della Volpe, Galvano, *Critica dell'ideologia contemporanea*, 1967.
2.18   Lotman, Jurij M., *The Structure of the Artistic Text*, Moscou 1970.

3. CZECH STRUCTURALISM

3.1   Faye, J.P. and Robel, L., 'Le cercle de Prague'. Special issue of the periodical *Change* (1969) No. 3.
3.2   Garwin, P.L., *A Prague Reader on Aesthetics, Literary Structure, and Style*, 1964.
3.3   Husserl, E., 'Briefe an Roman Ingarden', Den Haag 1968, *Phaenomenologica*, Vol. 25.
3.4   Mukařovský, J., *Kapitel aus der Poetik* (1948), Frankfurt 1967.
3.5   Mukařovský, J., *Kapitel aus der Aesthetik* (1966), Frankfurt 1970.
3.6   Patocka, J., *Edmund Husserl zum Gedächtnis*, Prague 1938.
3.7   Vachek, J. und Benes, E., *Stilistik und Soziolinguistik*, Beiträge der Prager Schule zur strukturellen Sprachbetrachtung und Spracherziehung, Berlin 1971.
3.8   Vachek, J., *The Linguistic School of Prague*, 1966.
3.9   Vachek, J.. *Prague School Reader in Linguistics*, 1964.

4. PARISIAN STRUCTURALISM

A. *Tel Quel*

4.1   'Théorie d'ensemble', *Tel Quel*, Paris 1968. (Contributions by Barthes, Foucault, Derrida, Kristeva, Ricardou, Sollers, Thibaudeau and others.)
4.2   Rehbein, I. (ed.), 'Revolutionäre Texttheorie: Die Gruppe Tel Quel', *Alternative* (1969) No. 66.

B. *Hermeneutics*

4.3   Gadamer, H.G., *Wahrheit und Methode*, Tübingen 1965.
4.4   Goldmann, L., *Marxisme et sciences humaines*, Paris 1970.
4.5   Goldmann, L., *Sciences humaines et philosophie*, Paris 1952.
4.6   Ricoeur, P., *De l'interprétation. Essai sur Freud*, Paris 1965.
4.7   Ricoeur, P., *Le conflit des interprétations. Essais d'herméneutique*, Paris 1969.

C. *Criticism*

4.8   Barthes, R., *Le degré zéro de l'écriture,* Paris 1953.
4.9   Barthes, R., *Sur Racine,* Paris 1964.
4.10 Barthes, R., *Essais Critiques,* Paris 1964.
4.11 Barthes, R., *Critique et vérité,* Paris 1966.
4.12 Barthes, R., *S/Z,* Paris 1970.
4.120 Barthes, R., *Sade, Fourier, Loyola,* Paris 1971.
4.121 Barthes, R., *Le Plaisir du texte,* Paris 1973.
4.13 Daix, P., *Nouvelle critique et art moderne,* Paris 1968.
4.14 Doubrovsky, S., *Pourquoi la nouvelle critique?* Paris 1967.
4.15 Dufrenne, M., *Pour l'homme,* Paris 1968.
4.16 Eco, U., *L'oeuvre ouverte,* Paris 1965.
4.160 Eco, U., *La structure absente,* Paris 1972.
4.17 Kristeva, J., *Semiotike. Recherches pour une sémanalyse,* Paris 1969.
4.170 Kristeva, J., 'Le sujet en procès', *Tel Quel,* No. 52 (1972) and 53 (1973).
4.18 Porle, R.C., 'Structuralism and Phenomenology: A Literary Approach', *The Journal of the British Society for Phenomenology,* **II**, 2 (1971).
4.19 Poulet, G., *Les chemins actuels de la critique,* Paris 1967.
4.20 Sollers, Ph., *Drame,* Paris 1965.
4.21 Sollers, Ph., *Logiques,* Paris 1968.
4.22 Sollers, Ph., *Nombres,* Paris 1968.
4.220 Sollers, Ph., *L'écriture et l'expérience des limites,* Paris 1968.

D. *Psychoanalysis*

4.23 *Cahiers pour l'analyse,* No. 3 (1969) (Cercle d'épistemologie de l'École Normale Supérieure, Paris) 'Sur l'objet de la psychoanalyse' (with contributions by Lacan, Green, Irigaray, Audouard, Milner.)
4.24 Castoriades-Aulagnier, P., 'Les constructions psychoanalytiques', *Topique,* Paris 1970, 3.
4.25 Fages, J.B., *Comprendre Jacques Lacan,* Paris 1971.
4.26 Freud, S., *Die Traumdeutung* (1900). Gesammelte Werke Vols. II, III.
4.27 Freud, S., *Konstruktionen in der Analyse,* 1937. Gesammelte Werke, Vol. XVI.
4.28 Lacan, J., *Écrits,* Paris 1966.
4.280 Lacan, J., *Les quatre concepts fondamentaux de la psychoanalyse. Le Séminaire, Livre XI,* Paris 1973.
4.29 Rifflet-Lemaire, A., *Jacques Lacan,* Brussels 1970.
4.290 Waelhens, A. de, *La psychose,* Paris/Louvain 1972.

E. *Structural Anthropology*

4.30 *Échanges et Communications.* Commemorative volume for Cl. Lévi-Strauss. Mouton, Den Haag 1970. Editors: J. Pouillon and P. Maranda, Vol. I, 706 pp., Vol. II, 746 pp. (This volume gives a good impression of the field and rich content of structural anthropology. The main works of Lévi-Strauss are the centre of the contribution. Authors are inter alia: Evans-Pritchard, Lévy, Hooper, Leiris, Benveniste, Jakobson, Haudricourt, Sebeok, Leach, Pouillon, Barthes, Todorov, Aron, Bastide, Vuillemin, Voegelin, Dumézil, Greimas)
4.31 Lévi-Strauss, Cl., *Les structures élémentaires de la parenté,* Paris 1949.
4.32 Lévi-Strauss, Cl., *Race et histoire,* Paris 1952.
4.33 Lévi-Strauss, Cl., *Tristes Tropiques,* Paris 1955.
4.34 Lévi-Strauss, Cl., *Anthropologie structurale,* Paris 1958.

4.35   Lévi-Strauss, Cl., *La pensée sauvage,* Paris 1962.
4.36   Lévi-Strauss, Cl., *Le totémisme d'aujourd'hui,* Paris 1962.
4.37   Lévi-Strauss, Cl., *Mythologies,* I (1964), II (1966), III (1968), IV (1971).
4.38   Charbonnier, G., *Entretiens avec Cl. Lévi-Strauss,* Paris 1961.
4.39   Derrida, J., 'Nature, Culture, Écriture. De Lévi-Strauss à Rousseau', *Cahiers pour l'analyse,* No. 4, 1970.
4.40   Geras, N.M., 'Lévy-Strauss and Philosophy', *The Journal of the British Society for Phenomenology,* I, 3 (1970).
4.400 Leach, E., *Lévi-Strauss,* London 1970.
4.41   Lepenies, W. and Ritter, H.H., *Orte des wilden Denkens,* Frankfurt 1970.
4.42   Lévi-Strauss, Cl., special issue of the periodical *L'Arc* No. 26, (1968).

F. *Philosophical Designs*

Grammatology

4.43   Derrida, J., *De la grammatologie,* Paris 1967.
4.44   Derrida, J., *La voix et le phénomène,* Paris 1967.
4.45   Derrida, J., *L'écriture et la différence,* Paris 1967.
4.46   Derrida, J., 'La mythologie blanche', *Poétique, revue de théorie et d'analyses littéraires* No. 5 (1971).
4.460 Derrida, J., *La dissémination,* Paris 1972.
4.461 Derrida, J., *Marges de la philosophie,* Paris 1972.
4.462 Derrida, J., *Positions,* Paris 1972.
4.47   Parret, H., 'Jacques Derrida. Een wijsbegeerte van de schriftuur', *Tijdschrift voor Filosofie* **XXX** (1968) 1.
4.470 Parret, H., 'Over de 'notie' van schriftuur', *Tijdschrift voor Filosofie* **XXXIV** (1972) 3.

Archeology

4.48   Foucault, M., *Maladie mentale et psychologie,* Paris 1961.
4.49   Foucault, M., *Histoire de la folie,* Paris 1961.
4.50   Foucault, M., *Naissance de la clinique,* Paris 1963.
4.51   Foucault, M., *Les mots et les choses,* Paris 1966.
4.52   Foucault, M., *L'archéologie du savoir,* Paris 1969.
4.53   Foucault, M., *L'ordre du discours,* Paris 1971.

Marxism

4.54   Althusser, L., *Pour Marx,* Paris 1965.
4.55   Althsser, L. (c.s.), *Lire le capital,* 2 Vols., Paris 1968.
4.56   Aron, R., *D'une sainte famille à l'autre,* Paris 1969.
4.57   Aron, R., *De la condition historique du sociologie,* Paris 1971.
4.58   Kosik, K., *Die Dialektik des Konkreten,* Frankfurt 1967.
4.59   Leduc, V., *Structuralisme et marxisme,* Paris 1970. (Contributions by Auzias, Canguilhem, Dufrenne, Goldmann, Lefebvre, Martinet, Mouloud *et al.*)
4.60   'La Pensée', special issue of the periodical *Structuralisme et marxisme* No. 135 (1967).
4.61   Sartre, J.P., *Critique de la raison dialectique,* Paris 1960.
4.62   Sartre, J.P., *L'idiot de la famille. Gustave Flaubert de 1821 à 1957.* 2 Vols., Paris 1971, 1972.
4.63   Sartre, J.P., special issue of the periodical *L'Arc* No. 30 (1966).
4.64   Schmidt, A., *Beiträge zur marxistischen Erkenntnistheorie,* Frankfurt 1969.
4.66   Stalin, J., 'Uber den Marxismus in der Sprachwissenschaft' (1950), in F.J. Raddatz (ed.), *Marxismus und Literatur* Vol. III, Hamburg 1969.

4.660 Gallas, H., *Strukturalismus als interpretatives Verfahren,* Darmstadt/Neuwied 1972.

5. THE PHILOSOPHY OF STRUCTURALISM

See Nos. *0.9; 1.4; 1.9; 4.5; 4.6; 4.7; 4.45; 4.51; 4.52; 4.53; 4.59; 4.66.*

Furthermore:

5.1 Ashby, W. Ross, *Design for a Brain,* New York 1952.
5.2 Broekman, Jan M., 'Filosofie van de kunst als filosofie van de ordening', *Algemeen Nederlands Tijdschrift voor Wijsbegeerte en Psychologie* **LVII** (1965) 4.
5.3 Carnap, R., *Der logische Aufbau der Welt,* Hamburg 1961.
5.4 Merleau-Ponty, M., *Signes,* Paris 1960.
5.5 Merleau-Ponty, M., *Éloge de la philosophie,* Paris 1965.
5.6 Nietzsche, F., *Werke* (ed. by K. Schlechta), Munchen 1958.
5.7 Wein, H., *Zugang zu philosophischer Kosmologie,* München 1954.
5.8 Wein, H., *Realdialektik,* Den Haag 1964.
5.9 Wilden, A., *System und Structure, Essays in Communication and Exchange,* London 1972.

INDEX OF NAMES

INDEX OF SUBJECTS

SYNTHESE LIBRARY

Monographs on Epistemology, Logic, Methodology,
Philosophy of Science, Sociology of Science and of Knowledge, and on the
Mathematical Methods of Social and Behavioral Sciences

Editors

ROBERT S. COHEN (Boston University)

DONALD DAVIDSON (The Rockefeller University and Princeton University)

JAAKKO HINTIKKA (Academy of Finland and Stanford University)

GABRIËL NUCHELMANS (University of Leyden)

WESLEY C. SALMON (University of Arizona)

15. C. D. BROAD, *Induction, Probability, and Causation. Selected Papers.* 1968, XI + 296 pp.
16. GÜNTHER PATZIG, *Aristotle's Theory of the Syllogism. A Logical-Philosophical Study of Book A of the Prior Analytics.* 1968, VXII + 215 pp.
17. NICHOLAS RESCHER, *Topics in Philosophical Logic.* 1968, XIV + 347 pp.
18. ROBERT S. COHEN and MARX W. WARTOFSKY (eds.), *Proceedings of the Boston Colloquium for the Philosophy of Science 1966–1968*, Boston Studies in the Philosophy of Science (ed. by Robert S. Cohen and Marx W. Wartofsky), Volume IV. 1969, VIII + 537 pp.
19. ROBERT S. COHEN and MARX W. WARTOFSKY (eds.), *Proceedings of the Boston Colloquium for the Philosophy of Science 1966–1968*, Boston Studies in the Philosophy of Science (ed. by Robert S. Cohen and Marx W. Wartofsky), Volume V. 1969, VIII + 482 pp.
20. J. W. DAVIS, D. J. HOCKNEY, and W. K. WILSON (eds.), *Philosophical Logic.* 1969, VIII + 277 pp.
21. D. DAVIDSON and J. HINTIKKA (eds.), *Words and Objections: Essays on the Work of W. V. Quine.* 1969, VIII + 366 pp.
22. PATRICK SUPPES, *Studies in the Methodology and Foundations of Science. Selected. Papers from 1911 to 1969*, XII + 473 pp.
23. JAAKKO HINTIKKA, *Models for Modalities. Selected Essays.* 1969, IX + 220 pp.
24. NICHOLAS RESCHER *et al.* (eds.). *Essay in Honor of Carl G. Hempel. A Tribute on the Occasion of his Sixty-Fifth Birthday.* 1969, VII + 272 pp.
25. P. V. TAVANEC (ed.), *Problems of the Logic of Scientific Knowledge.* 1969, XII + 429 pp.
26. MARSHALL SWAIN (ed.), *Induction, Acceptance, and Rational Belief.* 1970. VII + 232 pp.
27. ROBERT S. COHEN and RAYMOND J. SEEGER (eds.), *Ernst Mach; Physicist and Philosopher*, Boston Studies in the Philosophy of Science (ed. by Robert S. Cohen and Marx W. Wartofsky), Volume VI. 1970, VIII + 295 pp.
28. JAAKKO HINTIKKA and PATRICK SUPPES, *Information and Inference.* 1970, X + 336 pp.
29. KAREL LAMBERT, *Philosophical Problems in Logic. Some Recent Developments.* 1970, VII + 176 pp.
30. ROLF A. EBERKE, *Nominalistic Systems.* 1970, IX + 217 pp.
31. PAUL WEINGARTNER and GERHARD ZECHA (eds.), *Induction, Physics, and Ethics, Proceedings and Discussions of the 1968 Salzburg Colloquium in the Philosophy of Science.* 1970, X + 382 pp.
32. EVERT W. BETH, *Aspects of Modern Logic.* 1970, XI + 176 pp.
33. RISTO HILPINEN (ed.), *Deontic Logic: Introductory and Systematic Readings.* 1971, VII + 182 pp.
34. JEAN-LOUIS KRIVINE, *Introduction to Axiomatic Set Theory.* 1971. VII + 98 pp.
35. JOSEPH D. SNEED, *The Logical Structure of Mathematical Physics.* 1971, XV + 311 pp.
36. CARL R. KORDIG, *The Justification of Scientific Change.* 1971, XIV + 119 pp.
37. MILIČ ČAPEK, *Bergson and Modern Physics*, Boston Studies in the Philosophy of Science (ed. by Robert S. Cohen and Marx W. Wartofsky), Volume VII. 1971, XV + 414 pp.
38. NORWOOD RUSSELL HANSON, *What I do not Believe, and other Essays*, ed. by Stephen Toulmin and Harry Woolf. 1971, XII + 390 pp.

39. ROGER C. BUCK and ROBERT S. COHEN (eds.) *PSA 1970. In Memory of Rudolf Carnap*, Boston Studies in the Philosophy of Science (ed. by Robert S. Cohen and Marx W. Wartofsky), Volume VIII. 1971, LXVI + 615 pp. Also available as a paperback.
40. DONALD DAVIDSON and GILBERT HARMAN (eds.), *Semantics of Natural Language*. 1972, X + 769 pp. Also available as a paperback.
41. YEHOSUA BAR-HILLEL (ed.), *Pragmatics of Natural Language*. 1971, VII + 231 pp.
42. SÖREN STENLUND, *Combinators, λ-Terms and Proof Theory*. 1972, 184 pp.
43. MARTIN STRAUSS, *Modern Physics and Its Philosophy. Selected Papers in the Logic, History, and Philosophy of Science*. 1972, X + 297 pp.
44. MARIO BUNGE, *Method, Model and Matter*. 1973, VII + 196 pp.
45. MARIO BUNGE, *Philosophy of Physics*. 1973, IX + 248 pp.
46. A. A. ZINOV'EV, *Foundations of the Logical Theory of Scientific Knowledge (Complex Logic)*, Boston Studies in the Philosophy of Science (ed. by Robert S. Cohen and Marx W. Wartofsky), Volume IX. Revised and enlarged English edition with an appendix, by G. A. Smirnov, E. A. Sidorenka, A. M. Fedina, and L. A. Bobrova 1973, XXII + 301 pp. Also available as a paperback.
47. LADISLAV TONDL, *Scientific Procedures*, Boston Studies in the Philosophy of Science (ed. by Robert S. Cohen and Marx W. Wartofsky), Volume X. 1973, XII + 268 pp. Also available as a paperback.
48. NORWOOD RUSSELL HANSON, *Constellations and Conjectures*, ed. by Willard C. Humphreys, Jr. 1973, X + 282 pp.
49. K. J. J. HINTIKKA, J. M. E. MORAVCSIK, and P. SUPPES (eds.), *Approaches to Natural Language. Proceedings of the 1970 Stanford Workshop on Grammar and Semantics*. 1973, VIII + 526 pp. Also available as a paperback.
50. MARIO BUNGE (ed.), *Exact Philosophy – Problems, Tools, and Goals*. 1973, X+214 pp.
51. RADU J. BOGDAN and ILKKA NIINILUOTO (eds.), *Logic, Language, and Probability*. A selection of papers contributed to Sections IV, VI, and XI of the Fourth International Congress for Logic, Methodology, and Philosophy of Science, Bucharest, September 1971. 1973, X + 323 pp.
52. GLENN PEARCE and PATRICK MAYNARD (eds.), *Conceptual Chance*. 1973, XII + 282 pp.
53. ILKKA NIINILUOTO and RAIMO TUOMELA, *Theoretical Concepts and Hypothetico-Inductive Inference*. 1973. VII + 264 pp.
54. ROLAND FRAÏSSÉ, *Course of Mathematical Logic* – Volume I: *Relation and Logical Formula*. 1973, XVI + 186 pp. Also available as a paperback.
55. ADOLF GRÜNBAUM, *Philosophical Problems of Space and Time*. Second, enlarged edition, Boston Studies in the Philosophy of Science (ed. by Robert S. Cohen and Marx W. Wartofsky), Volume XII. 1973, XXIII + 884 pp. Also available as a paperback.
56. PATRICK SUPPES (ed.), *Space, Time, and Geometry*, 1973, XI + 424 pp.
57. HANS KELSEN, *Essays in Legal and Moral Philosophy*, selected and introduced by Ota Weinberger. 1973, XXVII + 300 pp.
58. R. J. SEEGER and ROBERT S. COHEN (eds.), *Philosophical Foundations of Science. Proceedings of an AAAS Program, 1969*. Boston Studies in the Philosophy of Science (ed. by Robert S. Cohen and Marx W. Wartofsky), Volume XI. 1974, X + 545 pp. Also available as paperback.
59. ROBERT S. COHEN and MARX W. WARTOFSKY (eds.), *Logical and Epistemological*

Studies in Contemporary Physics, Boston Studies in the Philosophy of Science (ed. by Robert S. Cohen and Marx W. Wartofsky), Volume XIII. 1973, VIII + 462 pp. Also available as a paperback.

60. ROBERT S. COHEN and MARX W. WARTOFSKY (eds.), *Methodological and Historical Essays in the Natural and Social Sciences. Proceedings of the Boston Colloquium for the Philosophy of Science, 1969–1972*, Boston Studies in the Philosophy of Science (ed. by Robert S. Cohen and Marx W. Wartofsky), Volume XIV. 1974, VIII + 405 pp. Also available as a paperback.

61. ROBERT S. COHEN, J. J. STACHEL, and MARX W. WARTOFSKY (eds.), *For Dirk Struik. Scientific, Historical and Political Essays in Honor of Dirk J. Struik*, Boston Studies in the Philosophy of Science (ed. by Robert S. Cohen and Marx W. Wartofsky), Volume XV. 1974, XXVII + 652 pp. Also available as a paperback.

62. KAZIMIERZ AJDUKIEWICZ, *Pragmatic Logic*, transl. from the Polish by Olgierd Wojtasiewicz.

63. SÖREN STENLUND (ed.), *Logical Theory and Semantic Analysis. Essays Dedicated to Stig Kanger on His Fiftieth Birthday*. 1974, V + 217 pp.

64. KENNETH F. SCHAFFNER and ROBERT S. COHEN (eds.), *Proceedings of the 1972 Biennial Meeting, Philosophy of Science Association*, Boston Studies in the Philosophy of Science (ed. by Robert S. Cohen and Marx W. Wartofsky), Volume XX. 1974, IX + 444 pp. Also available as a paperback.

65. HENRY E. KYBURG, JR., *The Logical Foundations of Statistical Inference*. 1974, IX + 421 pp.

66. MARJORIE GRENE, *The Understanding of Nature: Essays in the Philosophy of Biology*, Boston Studies in the Philosophy of Science (ed. by Robert S. Cohen and Marx W. Wartofsky), Volume XXIII. 1974, XII + 360 pp. Also available as a paperback.

67. JAN M. BROEKMAN, *Structuralism: Moscow, Prague, Paris*.

68. NORMAN GESCHWIND, *Selected Papers on Languge and the Brain*, Boston Studies in the Philosophy of Science (ed. by Robert S. Cohen and Marx W. Wartofsky), Volume XVI. 1974, XII + 549 pp. Also available as a paperback.

69. ROLAND FRAÏSSÉ, *Course of Mathematical Logic* – Volume II: Model Theory. 1974, XIX + 192 pp.

70. ANDRZEJ A. GREGORCZYK, *An Outline of Mathematical Logic*. Fundamental Results and Notions Explained with All Details. 1974, X + 596 pp.

SYNTHESE HISTORICAL LIBRARY

Texts and Studies
in the History of Logic and Philosophy

Editors:

N. KRETZMANN (Cornell University)
G. NUCHELMANS (University of Leyden)
L. M. DE RIJK (University of Leyden)

1. M. T. BEONIO-BROCCHIERI FUMAGALLI, *The Logic of Abelard.* Translated from the Italian. 1969, IX + 101 pp.
2. GOTTFRIED WILHELM LEIBNITZ, *Philosophical Papers and Letters.* A selection translated and edited, with an introduction, by Leroy E. Loemker. 1969, XII + 736 pp.
3. ERNST MALLY, *Logische Schriften*, ed. by Karl Wolf and Paul Weingartner. 1971, X + 340 pp.
4. LEWIS WHITE BECK (ed.), *Proceedings of the Third International Kant Congress.* 1972, XI + 718 pp.
5. BERNARD BOLZANO, *Theory of Science*, ed. by Jan Berg. 1973, XV + 398 pp.
6. J. M. E. MORAVCSIK (ed.), *Patterns in Plato's Thought. Papers arising out of the 1971 West Coast Greek Philosophy Conference.* 1973, VIII + 212 pp.
7. NABIL SHEHABY, *The Propositional Logic of Avicenna: A Translation from al-Shifā':al-Qiyās*, with Introduction, Commentary and Glossary. 1973, XIII + 296 pp.
8. DESMOND PAUL HENRY, *Commentary on De Grammatico: The Historical-Logical Dimensions of a Dialogue of St. Anselm's.* 1974, IX + 345 pp.
9. JOHN CORCORAN, *Ancient Logic and Its Modern Interpretations.* 1974. X + 208 pp.
10. E. M. BARTH, *The Logic of the Articles in Traditional Philosophy.* 1974, XXVII + + 533 pp.
11. JAAKKO HINTIKKA, *Knowledge and the Known. Historical Perspectives in Epistemology.* 1974, XII + 243 pp.
12. E. J. ASHWORTH, *Language and Logic in the Post-Medieval Period.* 1974, XIII + 304 pp.